UNDERCOVER AGENT

Undercover Agent

HOW ONE HONEST MAN TOOK
ON THE DRUG MOB...
AND THEN THE
MOUNTIES

Leonard Mitchell and Peter Rehak

A DOUGLAS GIBSON BOOK

M&S

Copyright © 1988 by Leonard Mitchell and Peter Rehak

Canadian Cataloguing in Publication Data

Mitchell, Leonard.
Undercover agent

ISBN 0-7710-6061-0

1. Mitchell, Leonard.   2. Undercover operations –
Nova Scotia – Lockeport.   3. Royal Canadian Mounted
Police.   4. Narcotics, Control of – Canada.
I. Rehak, Peter, 1936–   . II. Title.

HV8160.L6M58 1988   363.4'5'0924   C88-094325-4

Printed and Bound in Canada by Friesen Printers
Typesetting by Q Composition
Text design by Peter Maher
Cartography by Catherine Farley

A Douglas Gibson Book
McClelland and Stewart
The Canadian Publishers
481 University Avenue
Toronto M5G 2E9

To Robert Rueter,
a good lawyer, a great friend.

CONTENTS

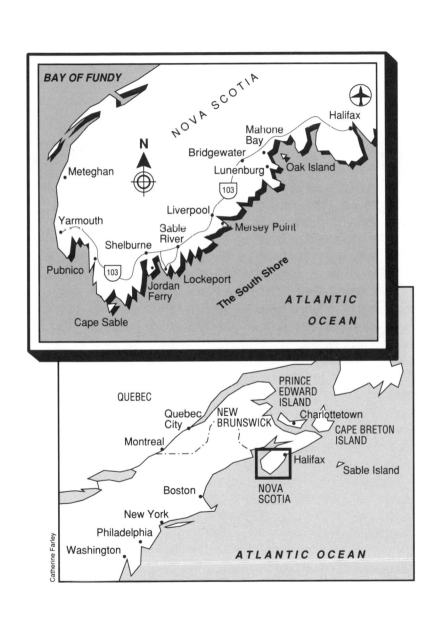

BAY OF FUNDY

NOVA SCOTIA

Halifax

Mahone
Bay

Bridgewater

N

Meteghan

Lunenburg

Oak Island

103

Liverpool

Yarmouth

Sable
River

Mersey Point

Shelburne

Pubnico

103

Lockeport

The South Shore

Jordan
Ferry

ATLANTIC

Cape Sable

OCEAN

QUEBEC

PRINCE
EDWARD
ISLAND

Quebec
City

NEW
BRUNSWICK

Charlottetown

Montreal

CAPE BRETON
ISLAND

Halifax

Boston

Sable Island

NOVA
SCOTIA

New York

Philadelphia

Washington

ATLANTIC OCEAN

Catherine Farley

CHAPTER ONE

An Unusual Deal

I'LL TELL YOU THE STORY JUST THE WAY IT HAPPENED.

It all began with a phone call about fish. It was an unusually hot day in May 1983, and I was unloading a heap of marine scrap at the yard when my wife phoned from home in Lockeport.

"Leonard, there are two fellows from Quebec here to see you, and they want to buy some fish. They say they want a lot of them and they're in a hurry. Can you meet them somewhere?"

"Sure. Tell them to wait at the Lockeport turnoff from the highway."

I jumped into the cab of my trusty old half-ton and drove off to meet the surprise visitors from Quebec.

For some years I'd been the proud owner of Shelburne Scrap and Metal in the town of Shelburne on Nova Scotia's South Shore. And to someone "from away" – as we call anyone from outside the string of towns and villages along the coast from Halifax down to Yarmouth that makes up the South Shore – it might have seemed strange to go to a scrap metal dealer for fish. But while the South Shore is one of the prettiest parts of North America, the economy has its ups and downs. So I've found it wise to have more than one iron in the fire. Besides the scrapyard I had a marine supply store and a bottle exchange going. And because I had spent five years as a fisherman, I couldn't give up my link with the sea. I kept my hand in as a fish broker, too. So the strangers who had driven to see Elaine at our house in Lockeport, twelve miles north of Shelburne, had come to the right place to buy fish. I was always ready to make a deal.

For more than a dozen years Elaine and I had built our lives on the South Shore and now had a home in Lockeport right on the edge of the Atlantic Ocean. She worked with me in the scrapyard and in the fish business along with her twin brother, Jim Dooks, who was also my partner. Our daughters, Sharon, fifteen, and Jewell, thirteen, had spent almost all their lives in Lockeport. Lockeport was home. We were happy and successful there, and we never thought we would have to leave. And I certainly didn't think that the meeting to which I headed up Highway 103 could set off a chain of events that would lead to our family being forced to leave town for a life spent on the run.

As I drove toward the Lockeport turnoff, I thought about how we had succeeded on the South Shore despite the fact that we were considered "from away" because our families hadn't lived there for generations. That both of us were born and raised in Oyster Pond Jeddore, a small community just east of Halifax, cut no ice in Lockeport.

It takes a long time to be accepted in a place like Lockeport, an island now joined by road to the mainland where people still talk about living "on town" and travelling "off town."

After more than ten years we were still regarded as outsiders even though I had a thriving business and a new house and our whole family was involved in the local Pentecostal Church. Elaine taught Sunday school for years and years, and as active Christians we all took part in a great many church activities.

I wasn't always religious. I've had my bouts with alcohol – I once had "a problem with my elbow," as they say here – and high living. But I chucked all that years ago, thanks to Elaine's good influence. I'm a better man for it, and I don't plan to change my ways now or in the future. I find that my beliefs give me some principles to live by, which helps when things get rough.

.   .   .

Lockeport's original settlers, Dr Jonathan Locke and Josiah Churchill, both from Massachusetts, were attracted to the site by the nearness of the world's richest fishing grounds. That was around 1760, and fishing has been the lifeblood of Lockeport ever since. Most people in town are either fishermen themselves or they work in one of the local fish-processing plants. Trawlers of all sizes chug their way across the harbour, taking their catch to one of the plants or to a broker at the wharf, under the eye of the huge old Locke mansion with its commanding view of the harbour. The Locke house has been left virtually intact since the 1800s, when Lockeport flourished thanks to the fishery and West Indian trade, which like the rest of Nova Scotia's trade in those days was conducted by "wooden ships and iron men."

Today, Lockeport's wealth is restricted to a handful of the population of roughly nine hundred, and the town's only visible connection with money is Crescent Beach, a mile-long stretch of unbroken white sand that until recently was depicted on the back of Canada's fifty-dollar bill. The beach is Lockeport's main landmark and reflects the wide range of coastal weather. On a warm summer day it can look like a beach in the Caribbean. But when an Atlantic storm moves in with a wind so sharp it would cut the whiskers right off your face, the waves breaking over the rocks make it an awe-inspiring sight.

In recent years the town has seen hard times. A fire that burned down its centre in 1975 has left it scarred to this day, so that only a few mixed-goods stores, a big drug store, and a federal building make up its "downtown." Elaine and I were relative newcomers when the fire hit, and I still remember the red glow and the desperate efforts of the fire brigade to prevent its spread. At other times both of the big fish plants – the giant Halifax-based National Sea and the Lockeport-based Pierce Fisheries – were also razed by fire, although they have now been rebuilt. But this is still an area where money is scarce, and anyone with money to spend is soon noticed.

•   •   •

Elaine and I came to Lockeport in the early seventies, when a new industry started – offshore lobster fishing. Lobster had been caught only inshore, close to the land, before someone had the smart idea of going out to sea to get them. Back then I had a part-time job at Lockeport's lighthouse at Gull Rock, and like any red-blooded, blue-nosed Nova Scotia boy I jumped at the chance to go to sea. I moved Elaine and the little girls down from Jeddore to our new life at Lockeport.

For five years I was a full-time fisherman, but I knew that I didn't want to spend the rest of my life going to sea. The commercial fishing season is in the winter months – for lobster it's November to May – and of course that's just when the North Atlantic is at its fiercest. Six of us used to stay out for a week, or even two, bouncing and tossing on a little trawler, its superstructure encrusted in ice that we had to chip off hour after hour to keep the top-heavy boat from turning turtle. In conditions like that it takes all the crew's strength just to haul in the catch and keep the gear in working order, and no one got much sleep. Not only is the work very hard, it's also dangerous. Just about every season a trawler doesn't make it back. In 1961 Lockeport was hit especially hard when three trawlers were lost in a late winter storm. Seventeen men died, leaving more than fifty children orphaned.

It's no wonder that Elaine and I often discussed various alternative business ventures we could get into. Through the years she has been a valuable partner in all my enterprises. She has shared in the work – at the scrapyard she kept the books, minded our money, and handled the phone – but she has also provided sober second thoughts. I don't think I would have been nearly as successful without her. I don't have much of a head for details, and I'm sometimes too impatient, some might even say reckless.

But I must confess that in my first venture into the scrap business I ignored her advice. During my occasional shopping trips to Shelburne and Halifax, I had noticed that there were quite a few scrap dealers around, and they appeared to be making a fair living selling scrap metal, batteries, copper, and so on, and these were things that were lying around everywhere. It seemed to me that wherever you went, you tripped over scrap metal that nobody was heeding. I smelled a business opportunity, and one February day I told Elaine that I was going to buy up some of this junk and resell it at a profit. We had about a thousand dollars in the bank, and I was planning to use it.

She told me to leave the money in the bank but after some thought I secretly decided to withdraw the money anyway. I took my old half-ton truck, bought up every piece of scrap that would fit onto it, and drove to Halifax. Prices for scrap were sky-high, and I made three thousand dollars profit on the first load.

"Maybe you've got something there," Elaine conceded once I got up my nerve to confess what I had done and she saw how successful I had been. After that she encouraged me to take more loads to Halifax, and before long, we had enough money to buy a one-ton truck.

That was the start of Shelburne Scrap and Metal, the company I founded and ran until Jim Dooks joined me when he left the army. But the sea was in my blood and I couldn't leave fishing altogether. Occasionally I went out on a boat, and later became a broker, selling other people's catches up and down the South Shore.

I was pretty well known in the area as a man who could hustle up a load of fish in a hurry or dispose of one with equal speed. That's why I wasn't surprised when Elaine called that day to tell me that two men from Quebec were looking for a load of fish. I didn't know then that the deal was destined to change my life.

•   •   •

I swung right at the Lockeport turnoff. Just off the highway in the shade of some trees was a bluish-grey Cadillac with Quebec licence plates. Two distinguished-looking middle-aged men were leaning against the car. They were wearing business suits, which made them stand out in a place like Lockeport, where work clothes were the order of the day. We shook hands, and in fluent but accented English they introduced themselves as André and Marcel Gélinas. They told me they were brothers and that they owned a restaurant in Montreal.

"We need a supply of fish," André said. "All kinds of fish — scallops, lobsters, cod, halibut. And we're looking for someone who can supply us steadily."

It was a tempting proposition, but I didn't see how I could do it. My fish deals were all local; I just used my old half-ton truck to buy from the local fishermen and take their catch to the fish plants along the South Shore. Montreal, by contrast, was nearly eight hundred miles away, and I would need a truck with a freezer unit to take a big load of fish there.

"I'm sorry, I can't help you," I told them. "I don't have a freezer truck, and I can't afford to buy one right now."

They seemed disappointed, but they didn't press me. We shot the breeze for a bit, then shook hands, got into our vehicles, and drove off in different directions. And I expected to hear no more about the Montreal fish deal.

•   •   •

But about a week later, the phone rang again and André at the other end said, "We've been thinking about it. We really need the fish badly. We're prepared to buy the truck – with a refrigerator unit and all."

All I had to do, they said, was pick up the truck, buy the fish, and bring the load to their restaurant. If things went well, I could buy the truck from them with the profit that I would make. I was startled. It was a very attractive deal, and I knew I'd be crazy as Luke's dog to turn it down. So I thought about it only briefly and then said, "Okay, I'll do it."

Right away I started to make phone calls to see who had some fish available. It didn't look too hard from my end. I knew every place on the South Shore where you could buy fish at a good price. After all, I bought and sold fish every day. Marcel and André's proposition looked like a good opportunity to expand my business, because I didn't have to worry about selling the fish in Montreal. Marcel and André wanted them. All I had to do was deliver the shipment where they told me to, collect my money, and laugh all the way to the bank.

It sounded good. Looking back on it, it sounded just a bit too good. And, as I've since learned, if it sounds too good to be true, it probably is.

A few days later I picked up the freezer truck in Dartmouth. They paid for it, and I brought it home. Working fast, I put together a load of fish worth about thirty thousand dollars, which I paid for myself, borrowing the money from the bank. I didn't have any trouble getting a loan, because my bank manager, Bill Sharpe, was used to my crazy business ventures by now. Just the same, thirty thousand dollars was a lot of money to me. More than I could afford to lose.

It was unusually hot – even on the South Shore – when I set out for Montreal in the last week of May. Just before I climbed into the new truck, I called André and told him I was on my way with the load of fish as we had agreed. He said, "That's fine." He sounded happy.

The heat wave stayed with me throughout the trip. It was

17

a long haul up to Halifax, and then the long haul along the Trans-Canada Highway across Nova Scotia and New Brunswick and into Quebec. I had made the trip to Montreal a few times before, but always in a car or small truck. The refrigerated truck was big and bulky and slow, and the hours crawled by. As I drove past Quebec City, André met me in the Cadillac. He said I should follow him to Montreal, to the restaurant. So I drove behind him all the way. All in all, it took me nearly twenty-four hours on the road to get to the outskirts of Montreal.

At last André pulled up to a restaurant. It was a really nice-looking place, I think on Decarie Boulevard, and we drove around the back to the receiving area. The chef and an assistant came out and looked at the fish. They bought a few boxes. Not a lot. That was a surprise. Even worse, I was getting the impression that André didn't own the restaurant. He just seemed to know these people. Then I noticed that he was phoning other places to try to sell the rest of the load. Suddenly it dawned on me that the fish had not been sold in advance. I got butterflies in my stomach. I had thirty thousand bucks invested in that load, and I could sense that there could be problems getting rid of it.

But André and Marcel just kept saying, "Don't worry. Everything is all right."

As you can imagine, I wasn't very comforted by their assurances. And I had reason to be worried. One thing about the fish trade is that you have to move the goods or they'll spoil — and very quickly. A rotting fish is about as easy to sell as typhoid. I was doubly worried because we were in Montreal. On my home turf in the Maritimes I can sell anything, and I could certainly have disposed of a load of fish quite easily. But here on the streets of Montreal I was for all practical purposes in a foreign country. For one thing, I couldn't speak French, and it's hard to sell stuff when you don't know the language. I suppose there are some people who can do such things, but I'm not one of them.

Also, in Montreal it was really hot, hot enough to fry eggs on the sidewalk. I had to have the refrigeration unit on all the time, roaring away, but from the first day I was worried that the whole load would spoil before we could sell it.

It was obvious that we would have to be around for a few days. At this point it turned out that Marcel and André lived in Quebec City – another nasty surprise – and we all checked into a hotel on Sherbrooke Street. For five or six days they were on the phone trying to sell the fish, setting up appointments for us to trail around to various restaurants. It got to be sort of a routine. Each day I'd say, "Where are we going next with the fish?" Then we'd drive around Montreal, and people they knew would buy fish in small quantities.

This went on for three or four days, and the fish were getting older every day. We must have called on a hundred restaurants, but although we were getting rid of some fish, the pace wasn't fast enough to make me feel comfortable, and I was really worried. I called Elaine one night to confess.

"Listen," I told her, "of all the things I've done this is really a good one. We could lose the house and everything, our life savings. This is turning into a nightmare."

I was puzzled. I couldn't figure out why the two brothers would go to so much trouble to get this shipment organized and then have so much difficulty in selling it. I didn't spend too much time thinking about it, though. My first priority was to get rid of the fish and recover my investment. That kept me too busy to make any detailed analysis.

The hotel was comfortable enough. I had a room to myself, while André and Marcel shared a room down the hall. I noticed that they were surrounded by a lot of activity. People would come and go to their room, and sometimes I would see them visiting other rooms in the hotel. To me they would say: "That guy is helping us sell the fish. He knows everybody. We're putting it together."

I wasn't paying too much attention to the people going in and out. Although I met some of them, I didn't retain their names. I'm bad about names under any circumstances, and I was really worried about my thirty thousand bucks worth of fish out there in the truck with the refrigeration unit blasting away night and day. In the end we dropped the price drastically and set off on a new sales round. It took us another five days, but we finally sold the whole load. I lost about fifteen hundred dollars on the deal.

Needless to say, I told André and Marcel that I'd take no more fish to Montreal, and I headed east down the Trans-Canada for the coolness of home. But about a week later they phoned me, asking for more fish. I really didn't understand it and told them straight out: "Look, I lost money on that first shipment, and there's no way I'm going to go through all that again. The business isn't going to work. You better come and get your truck."

A few days later they showed up in the Cadillac. This time they had a driver with them, and he drove off in the refrig-erator truck. I was sorry to see it go, because I had always wanted one, but I couldn't see any way to make this business work.

It was certainly a strange episode. To this day I haven't figured out why they went to all that trouble, coming all the way to Lockeport and making such a fuss about needing the fish, and then not having them sold ahead of time. They, too, had an investment in the venture – the truck – and to be fair they and their mysterious friends spent a great deal of time trying to make it all work out.

It was all very strange. And they didn't look like incom-petent men.

CHAPTER TWO

A
Natural
Place

I DON'T KNOW WHAT ATTRACTED THEM TO ME, BUT MARCEL AND
André kept calling during the month that followed that trip
to Montreal. Usually they spoke to Elaine and tried to talk
her – and me – into another fish deal. On one occasion, unless
Elaine was hearing things, they tried to sell me a trailer-truck-
load of slippers. I never returned any of the calls, but that
didn't seem to bother them, and they just kept on calling.

One day a new man called. He said his name was John
O'Carroll and that he was a friend of the Gélinas brothers.
He told Elaine: "I'm coming down to Lockeport with some
friends of mine, and I'd like your husband to pick us up at
the airport in Halifax."

Forget it, I thought. I didn't see any point in making the

two-and-a-half-hour drive to the Halifax airport. I had no idea who John O'Carroll was, and since he was referred to me by the Gélinas brothers I assumed that he was looking for another fish deal. And I certainly wasn't going to bite.

The next day – it was in October, but I've forgotten the exact date – O'Carroll called from the Halifax airport and ranted and raved at Elaine, who as usual was on phone duty at home in Lockeport.

"Where the devil is your husband? Didn't I ask him to pick me up?"

Elaine did her best to settle him down, pointing out that I never did agree to meet him. In the end he calmed down enough to say, "We're renting a car and we'll drive down to Lockeport. How do we find your house?"

Elaine told him that our house was hard to find and suggested that he wait for me just off Highway 103 at Sable River. This was a crossroads that was well marked and easy to find. "Leonard will meet you there," she told him, and he agreed.

When Elaine phoned the scrapyard she was told that I was out making a fish deal. She eventually tracked me down at a local fish plant and said, "You better go to meet those people. They gave me a hard time on the phone, so you better find out what they want."

She told me they expected to reach the crossroads around one or two o'clock that afternoon. This left me plenty of time to complete the deal I was working on and to drop by Shelburne Scrap and Metal to see how Jim Dooks was doing. Jim, a good-humoured bear of a man, did most of the work inside the yard while I travelled around drumming up new business and looking after the actual wheeling and dealing, since Jim didn't have much experience or inclination for that sort of thing.

When I got to the crossroads the visitors were already there, in a big rented American car of the type we call a 'snowbanker' for obvious reasons. Once I saw O'Carroll I remembered him as one of the men I'd seen going in and out of the Gélinas brothers' hotel room in Montreal. He was a tall, burly man with a full head of reddish-blond hair, a gruff, tough-looking guy. He appeared to be in his fifties. As he puffed away at a cigarette, I noticed that his hands were scarred around the knuckles. With him were three men, all dressed very casually in jeans and sportshirts, as if they were on vacation. But there was something different about them, something that made me uneasy.

One, introduced as Irving, said he was O'Carroll's brother-in-law. He was not quite six feet tall and had short, dark hair. It soon became clear that when O'Carroll barked, Irving jumped. And sometimes O'Carroll barked.

The other two men were from Miami. One was a distinguished-looking guy with grey hair. He said his name was Kanoski. He had a gold chain around his neck and fancy gold rings, one of them with a lion's head on it.

The other man from Miami was Rod. He was around thirty and at least six-foot-two or six-foot-three and very skinny, with high cheekbones that gave him a lean and hungry hawk-like look. He had curly reddish-blond hair, which he wore three-quarter length. Like the others, he was casually dressed in blue jeans, a sportshirt, and a light jacket. He also wore a striking pair of moccasins. They were hand-sewn of real leather. I'm no expert, but they looked like they came from South America or from real Indian country in the States, Arizona, or New Mexico.

They were certainly an odd-looking bunch. I didn't think I'd have any interest in whatever proposition they were about to make, since I was sure it involved another fish deal. Just meeting them left me anxious to spend as little time as possible with these guys.

But O'Carroll had other ideas.

"Can we go somewhere to get something to eat as well as talk?" he asked as soon as the introductions were made. There was something strange even in the way he introduced me. I never actually met O'Carroll in Montreal, though I did see him. Yet now he was behaving as if we knew each other from way back. Although I was uneasy, it seemed rude not to accept their invitation, so I got into their car. O'Carroll drove and Irving sat beside him. I found myself in the back seat with Rod and Kanoski. I'm a big man – six-foot-one and nearly four hundred pounds – so, as you can imagine, we were pretty cramped.

"Drive south. We'll go to Barrington," I said. "There's a good restaurant there called the Seabreeze."

Barrington was about an hour's drive, and I presumed this would give us a chance to talk on the way. I don't like discussing business in restaurants. In a small community like Lockeport, or even Shelburne, people have big ears, and an overheard conversation can easily ruin a deal. My wheelings and dealings attracted plenty of gossip anyway, and I didn't want to add grist to the mill. But even sitting there wedged between these two cool customers from Miami, I still didn't suspect that there might be a real need for secrecy.

O'Carroll, still smoking, with his big scarred hands on the wheel, didn't waste any time getting to the point. "Rod here is big in the drug trade," he said. "He's from Miami, and things are getting hot down there. So he'd like to bring in some of his stuff through Canada, and Nova Scotia's the best bet. We'd like to use your boat – and we'd make it worth your while. We're talking big money."

I couldn't believe my ears. It was like being part of a movie or a bad dream. In the car they were all staring at me, and I could barely get out the words to say that I didn't own a boat. Sure, I was in the business of buying and selling fish, I explained, but I had given up going to sea myself long ago. As I spoke, I racked my brain for a clue as to why this group was making this proposition to me, an ordinary guy who had never been in trouble with the law.

The worst thing about the whole crazy set-up was that it wasn't even really a proposition. They never asked me whether I was interested in the deal, or whether I would do it. They just assumed from the start that everything had been settled and that there was no question about my taking part. And as the conversation went on, with them explaining that they'd do this and I'd do that, it got harder to say no to this carload of mobsters driving me down a lonely highway.

It became clear to me that O'Carroll had led Rod to believe that I had a boat and that I was ready to jump at any illegal business proposition, especially one that would leave me "fat," as they said. They mentioned millions of dollars. Whenever I said that I didn't have a boat and that I had no idea where I would get one, O'Carroll would quickly jump in and say, "He has access to a boat," or "It's just a matter of working out the details."

I was dazed by all this, but sensing that I couldn't show it, I decided to play along, trying to say as little as possible beyond making it clear I didn't have a boat. From the way they were talking, the shipment was expected within a month, and they wanted to get everything sorted out quickly.

"We need a good-quality boat, one with a steel hull," Rod announced, and Irving, who surfaced as the group's transportation expert, nodded.

By the time we got to the Seabreeze, they felt able to switch to discussing innocuous things over lunch. As far as they were concerned, it was all cut and dried. I was their man — the fact that I had no criminal record and had a good reputation was just what they wanted — and all that remained to be worked out were some small details – like the boat. That was the general tone.

It was now clear to me that Rod, who followed the conversation keenly, his hawk-like eyes jumping from speaker to speaker, was the man in charge. This was his project. O'Carroll was making the introductions and would be a mere liaison man, the Montreal connection. He would keep in touch with me by phone and would pass on Rod's instructions.

During the drive back to Sable River, Rod, who was sitting beside me in the back seat, made it clear that we were all in this together. Without any warning, he turned to me and said, "If anything goes wrong, you'll read about it in the papers.

Everyone goes down. If anyone's name is not in the papers,"
– and here he made a point with his finger like a gun and
aimed it at me – "Bang. You bite the dust.

"You know what I'm saying?" he asked. "I'm saying that if
we should get caught with the goods, everybody takes the
fall."

It couldn't have been any clearer.

As they dropped me off and drove away, I was still trying
to figure out why they had approached *me*. I knew for sure
that I would never go along with the scheme, millions or no
millions, and I'd have to figure out how to get out of it.

·   ·   ·

Elaine was stunned when I told her what had happened. "There's
no way we can do anything else except go to the RCMP," she
said.

I had already decided that; I just wanted her reassurance
that my instinct was right. This could become dangerous, and
I wanted to be sure that she agreed with me. We decided
that I would go to the Mounties the very next day.

All of that evening and long into the night we speculated
about why on earth the drug smugglers had picked me to
help them. There was no question that the Gélinas brothers
had directed O'Carroll to me. (The police later told me that
O'Carroll was a well-known figure on the Montreal organized
crime scene and that at least one of the Gélinas brothers was
also involved.) But I never noticed anything unusual while I
was with them in Montreal. There wasn't even a hint of drugs
while we were selling the fish. The fish enterprise, however
crazy it may have been, was completely legitimate.

Friends have suggested to me that the brothers were testing
the waters for the drug smugglers, that they wanted to see
what I was like. It's also been suggested that they were trying
to get me into debt so that a drug deal would be even more
attractive to me. I can't buy either of those theories. Nothing
was mentioned during the fish episode that even hinted at

an illegal deal down the road. And if they were supposed to be bankrupting me, they wouldn't have tried as hard as they did to sell all the fish.

The only plausible explanation is that O'Carroll was asked by mobster colleagues in Florida to recommend someone on Canada's east coast. He wasn't going to admit that he didn't really know anyone, so, eager to be the big shot, he recommended me, thinking that since he'd seen me with the Gélinas brothers I was either a criminal or a businessman in search of a fast buck.

He certainly never checked me out. And that, in the million-dollar world of drug smuggling, was a very expensive mistake.

•   •   •

I gather that there were plenty of good reasons why drug smugglers from Florida – the bad guys portrayed every week on "Miami Vice" – would be looking north. Their traditional route for importing the stuff — the coast of South Florida – had become threatened. During 1983 the Reagan Administration had stepped up its anti-drug activity. Coast Guard patrols had been reinforced and the Drug Enforcement Administration given more money and men to fight the importers.

That's why Rod and his Miami associates had turned for help to the Montreal mobsters who handled their distribution in that city. And O'Carroll, out to impress Rod and his associates, had got careless.

Nova Scotia was a natural choice for a smuggling operation. The jagged, finger-like coast, with more hidden bays than fleas on a dog's back, is next to impossible to watch properly. And it has a long tradition of smuggling. People on the South Shore have never been overly fond of government rules and regulations ("that fellow has the gall of the government" is a common expression among old-timers), so from the eighteenth century on everyone has smuggled whatever they could, whether it was rum from the Caribbean ("Lunenburg

Champagne") or manufactured goods from "the Boston states." Smuggling is part of the local heritage, you might say, and many a Nova Scotia fortune was made during Prohibition.

More recently, the South Shore gained international notoriety when 174 Sikhs, all illegal immigrants, landed on a rocky beach near Woods Harbour in the summer of 1987. A Spanish freighter brought them close enough to the coastline that they could wade ashore. That's some smart navigation, because the coastline around there is pretty tricky, unless you're the finest kind of skipper. Some local people believe that the only reason the episode surfaced was that the unfortunate Sikhs missed their pick-up point by taking a wrong turn when they got to the highway. A lot of strange cube vans were seen in the area on the Sunday they arrived, and some believe they were supposed to whisk the Sikhs to Toronto or Montreal. Again, no evidence was ever found. But then, no one has ever explained where the Sikhs' wives and children got to. Some locals think they arrived earlier without being noticed. The truth may never be known.

I've also thought that this was no isolated incident. There are so many nooks and crannies along the coast that anyone can bring in anything he wants. The RCMP has no patrol boats, and the Canadian Coast Guard and Armed Forces patrols are few and far between.

I only mention all this to show you that it all made sense as far as the drug smugglers were concerned. Nova Scotia was the natural place for crooks looking to establish a drug pipeline into Canada. The big mistake they made was choosing me.

While I don't drink anymore, I might have been tempted to smuggle some booze into the U.S. back in the 1920s, for in those days that was regarded as a very profitable and natural piece of neighbourliness, since most Canadians thought the Americans were crazy to outlaw drinking. Smuggling something that was legal at home was okay. But smuggling people or drugs is another matter. I hate the idea. I know what drug

addiction can do to people, especially teenagers. I kept thinking of my daughters, Jewell and Sharon, both teenagers. That's
why I knew I'd never go along with the smugglers. But I
didn't know how to get out of this crazy and dangerous situation.

At eight-thirty the morning after my meeting with O'Carroll
and his associates, I paid a call on the RCMP detachment in
Shelburne. Sergeant Gene Anderson listened to my story with
apparent interest and said: "What you're telling me is out of
our line of work here. We don't handle drug enforcement.
There's a special squad for that in Yarmouth. I'll call them.
They'll be in touch with you shortly."

About three days later, Constable Chris Paley of the Yarmouth Drug Squad phoned me and said he was in Halifax and
would like to stop by in Lockeport to see me on his way back
to Yarmouth. We agreed to meet at the very same crossroads
where I'd had my encounter with the drug smugglers.

I set out in the late afternoon. It's a short but scenic drive.
After you cross the open stretch alongside Crescent Beach,
the road from Lockeport to the highway is flanked by trees
on both sides, and they were now in their October colours.
The beauty of the scenery raised my hopes that an experienced RCMP officer would know how to get me out of this
situation.

It was getting dark when I reached the meeting place and
parked my Chevy half-ton off the road. A few minutes later
a "Plain Jane" Pontiac Bonneville, an undercover car, drove
up, and a man got out. Chris Paley didn't look like a Mountie.
He was about six feet tall and muscular, but he wore scholarly
horn-rimmed glasses with fairly thick lenses. He was dressed
in a T-shirt and corduroys and looked a bit sloppy, which no
doubt made him an effective undercover man. I liked him
instantly.

We drove off in his car, and I told him my story. Then it
went back and forth for about three-quarters of an hour as
he asked me question after question. We covered the waterfront from the fish deal to details of the meeting and back

again. Finally he said: "It sounds crazy, but I believe you. I don't know whether my superiors will or not. Would you agree to take a polygraph test?"

I said, "Yeah, I'll take a polygraph test."

"I'll be back to you within a day or two," he told me as he dropped me off next to my truck.

I heard later that Chris reported our conversation to his superiors in Yarmouth. They took my tale to the more senior brass in Halifax, who thrashed it out and decided that they should use me to find out more about the proposed operation. I guess they believed me, too, because I was never asked to take the polygraph test.

Some time later Chris was sent to ask me whether I would be willing to play along with the smugglers "just to see what happens." I know it sounds dumb now, but I was intrigued. It didn't look like it would be a lot of trouble. I thought perhaps there would be a meeting or two and a few phone calls, just a little bit of variety from buying fish and dealing scrap.

The Mounties must have thought the same thing. They were interested, but not sure whether the investigation would lead anywhere. Chris told me that they received a great many tips about drug deals, but only a few of them ever came to anything.

Looking back, it's amazing how lightly I took the decision. At the time I didn't have my heart set on nailing the smugglers or anything like that. Had the Mounties told me to tell O'Carroll to go away and not bother me again, I'd have done it without hesitation. But they didn't, and I didn't mind that either. I liked Chris Paley a lot, and I thought if I could be a good public-spirited citizen and help the Mounties, why not?

So I said yes, I'd play along with the drug smugglers, "just to see what happens."

•   •   •

The first step the RCMP took was to tap our phone. Chris Paley met me just outside the town of Pubnico near his base in Yarmouth, and I signed the consent forms laid out on the roof of his car. I had to do it twice; they lost the first ones, which wasn't encouraging.

Nothing happened for weeks and I almost forgot about the whole thing, even the phone tap. Then, out of the blue, John O'Carroll phoned.

"I heard from Rod," the gruff voice said. "Things are happening, and I'll be in touch with you soon again."

He left a Montreal number in case I needed him, and that was that. I took down the number and phoned Chris Paley. When another week went by, Chris phoned me. "Why don't you give O'Carroll a buzz and see if anything is shaking."

It turned out the number O'Carroll had left belonged to the hotel on Sherbrooke Street where I had stayed during the fish deal. He came to the phone, and as soon as I gave my name he rasped: "I'll call you back."

He did – the next day – and said he hadn't heard from Rod but that he expected things to start moving soon.

This was the start of a telephone tag routine that lasted for the next few months. I would call O'Carroll at the hotel, but he would never talk from there. He'd promise to get back to me and then would call from a pay phone. There was always a gap between my call and his return call. Sometimes the gap would be a day; at other times he wouldn't get back to me for two weeks. This made the RCMP's monitoring difficult, and Chris urged me from the start to try and get a definite time for the calls.

"Give me a time when you're going to call," I'd tell O'Carroll. "I move around a lot and I want to be sure that we connect."

This made it easier for the Mounties listening in, but O'Carroll didn't always stick to the agreed times. I don't know whether he was just busy or whether it was part of his personal precautions against being bugged by the police.

The RCMP were monitoring the calls from the Drug Squad offices in Yarmouth. I was now phoning them more often as well, calling Chris after every contact just to make sure he didn't miss a call. The Yarmouth office had installed a special phone – a private line – just for my calls. I had insisted on that because as the calls became more frequent I had trouble getting in touch with Chris. I was given an informal code name, Levi, in honour of the Levis jeans I wore a great deal of the time. I certainly received quick service whenever I phoned in and said, "Levi calling. Let me speak to Chris."

No action, just phone calls for a few more weeks until suddenly, just after Christmas 1983, O'Carroll called again and announced: "Things are almost ready to roll. We have to have a boat and we have to have a captain. Get moving on both."

It was almost two months to the day after the Miami and Montreal mob had taken me for a ride, and for the first time it looked like something was actually going to happen.

I called Chris Paley with the news.

"That's terrific. Good luck and keep us posted," he said, sounding excited.

I made the rounds of the boatyards until I found a vessel for sale in Pubnico that I thought could do the job. The *Endeavour* was a big boat, about ninety-five feet long, but she had a wooden hull. Rod had specified that the boat should have a steel hull. Wooden hulls were too vulnerable to damage in bad weather, he said. But I thought the *Endeavour* was sturdy enough to carry out the mission. I called O'Carroll.

"We'll come down and have a look," he said in his usual gruff manner.

A few days later they showed up. There was O'Carroll, Rod, and an engineer they called Charlie. I learned that Charlie was an expert in barge towing, but that he spent so much time checking out vessels for people in the drug smuggling business that it had almost become his main job. He told me he travelled wherever the mobsters operated and assessed whether the vessels they might use were up to the task of transporting the valuable cargo. He was a personable guy, very pleasant, and I was impressed with the technical knowledge he displayed.

With her owner-skipper at the wheel, we took the *Endea-*

vour out for a trial run around Pubnico harbour. While O'Carroll and Rod and I watched, Charlie paced the deck a bit and leaned over her gunwale to finger her wooden hull. I could tell that it was bothering him. Our spin around the harbour lasted about an hour. We docked and thanked the owner.

"She won't do," Charlie said when we got back in the car. "We've got to have a steel hull." He explained that they'd had bad experiences with wooden boats. Some of them had broken up in rough seas or while offloading from the larger mother ships, usually small freighters. These mother ships, I learned, ferried the drugs from South America and the Middle East, and it was the smaller ships, like the one we were looking for, that brought the cargo to shore. The contraband cargo was secretly transferred at sea, often in bad weather. Usually the ships tied up alongside one another, hull rubbing against hull, and this, Charlie explained, was rough on the smaller vessels whenever there was a sea on.

"A wooden hull can't take that kind of pressure. It can break up if the ships rub against one another. Then we lose the whole cargo. It's happened to us already, and that's why we have to have a steel hull."

I was now becoming aware that this was major-league stuff, that drug smuggling was a highly organized giant business, a huge corporation that had procedures and specifications for everything, even down to the ships they used. And the *Endeavour* didn't meet those specs.

I took Charlie's speech to heart, but the only South Shore boat with a steel hull that I knew was for sale was tied up in Shelburne. I took the group to see her. To me the *Lady Ann* looked like a bucket of rust. She'd been sitting at the berth for over two years. After a local man couldn't get a fishing licence for her she'd been taken back by the Fishermen's Loan Board.

Though I didn't think very much of the *Lady Ann*, this Charlie guy could see an awful lot of potential in her and said that if she were in shape, she could do the job.

Charlie and O'Carroll left in their car for Halifax, and Rod asked me to drive him to Yarmouth, where he was catching a plane for Boston and then going on to Miami. When we climbed into my truck he looked at me hard and made a startling announcement: "From now on you'll be dealing with me directly. I'll be calling you myself to give you instructions. O'Carroll is out of the picture on this one."

He didn't go into details, but he made it clear that he wasn't pleased with some of the things that had been happening through the Montreal connection. I had sensed from the beginning that the Montreal people were more interested in impressing Rod than in doing business. The way they told him at the outset that I had a boat was a perfect example. Later I heard that O'Carroll, who smoked constantly and seemed to be coughing more and more, was not well. He was said to have serious problems with his lungs, and that may also have affected Rod's decision.

In any case the new development worried me. While it now looked like the operation was getting into gear, and so might soon be over, it also moved the danger factor up a notch. I was now dealing directly with a sophisticated Miami drug ring, and I had to presume that they were a much rougher bunch than the Montreal underworld. And the traditional mobsters in that city were no slouches, either, when it came to settling scores.

If Rod wasn't happy with O'Carroll's performance so far, what was going to happen when he found out *my* real role in this enterprise?

CHAPTER THREE

The Mastermind

WHEN I REPORTED TO CHRIS PALEY THAT ROD HAD TAKEN OVER the operation, the Mounties sat up and took notice. Two additional RCMP drug squad officers joined Chris Paley on the case. They were Sergeant Brent Crowhurst, who was named strike co-ordinator, and Phil Pitts, a corporal who was Paley's superior. Paley and Pitts now functioned as partners, and I started to meet with both of them.

Things started happening in Miami, too. The RCMP had a man permanently stationed at the U.S. Drug Enforcement Administration (DEA) office there. In recent years Miami had become the funnel to the North American market for the continent's major drug dealers, and so many investigations in Canada had led to the drug subculture in South Florida that the RCMP found it expedient to have a man on the ground.

A DEA agent named Billy Yout, an affable and dedicated law enforcement officer, was the liaison man with the Miami-based Mountie. Now that Rod had taken the helm, the DEA became involved, although I didn't know this until later. Yout, a chunky guy with a moustache, decided to tackle the task of checking on Rod himself. There wasn't much to go on except the name Rod and whatever details were passed on to Miami through Chris Paley.

"We'd run surveillance on him from Canada down to Miami or Fort Lauderdale, and he'd be very elusive," Yout recalled later. "He'd get off a plane and we'd follow him — and we couldn't pin him down because he'd lose us."

Rod didn't suspect that he was being followed. It was just that he took evasive measures as part of his everyday routine — much like an intelligence agent in an unfriendly country. After spending many hours on his tail, even Billy Yout, a Florida-based cop experienced in tailing all sorts of hoods, found him "spooky."

He also found Rod's case unusual because most known drug traffickers in Miami were Latin Americans or Americans of Latin American origin, and the trade's language was Spanish. Rod, with his reddish-blond curls and his Florida accent, didn't fit that mould, and he hadn't previously attracted the DEA's attention.

My involvement in the case made the investigation more difficult. I was the only person that Rod was dealing with in Canada, and both the RCMP and the DEA decided early on that they would go to great lengths to protect my undercover role.

"We were very conservative in our investigative efforts. We had to keep our distance," Billy Yout recalled. "We re-alized that Leonard, as a legitimate businessman, was making tremendous sacrifices along with his family. We and the RCMP felt that we had a real responsibility to keep him from being compromised."

For example, the DEA or the Mounties could have identified Rod sooner if they had stopped him at an airport on the pretext of a customs violation. They feared, however, that they would blow my cover and ruin the case as well, because, as Yout said, "Rod was very bright and he would have quickly known what was up. In trying to protect Leonard we did a lot of things we would normally not have done. One time," Yout recalled, "we followed him to North Miami Beach. He went into a house and – Boom! – he never came out. He either went out the back door or jumped in a car somewhere."

But bit by bit Yout's doggedness started to pay off. Rod had given me a telephone number in Miami that I used to contact him. It turned out to be a pay phone in a gas station on one of the little islands off the MacArthur Causeway that spans Biscayne Bay, connecting Miami proper with Miami Beach. Yout and a team of agents staked out the gas station at a time when we had arranged to phone each other.

"Rod showed up but we couldn't get close enough," Yout remembered. "It was a pretty busy area and there were several different entrances. We tailed him when he left, but he didn't go back to wherever he lived – we still didn't know where his house was. He drove to Miami Beach and all the way to Fort Lauderdale before we lost him. He was good, really good. I couldn't keep up with him without burning him. I had my whole group out there on a number of occasions. We even had piggyback cars. But the way he drove, it was tough staying with him."

The DEA photographed him, but unless they could attach a name to the hawk-like face, the photos weren't much use. Billy Yout was getting more and more frustrated. One day there was a lucky break.

"He came back from Canada again, got off the plane at Fort Lauderdale, and took a cab to Miami. That's about thirty-five miles, and it would have been easier if he had flown into Miami, but he didn't. All of a sudden he stopped the cab in the middle of a street down by Biscayne Boulevard and jumped into a waiting Mercedes, a big Mercedes. We called in the licence, and it was registered to someone in Panama City in the Florida panhandle. That made it even more confusing. But we stayed on his tail and the car dropped him off in what turned out to be the general area of his house."

Yout and his agents followed Rod down the road where the Mercedes had let him off, but they lost him again. The next day the DEA ran property checks on thirty to forty houses in the area and came up with the name R. O'Dare. When the first name turned out to be Rory, Yout said to himself, "There goes my Rod theory." It didn't dawn on him at the time that "Rod" was the combination of Rory O'Dare's initials. When he started looking over the houses again, a couple looked like good prospects, but he decided to concentrate on O'Dare and his lavish house in the exclusive neighbourhood.

"We put surveillance on the house and never once saw him coming or going," Yout said. "There was a very attractive young lady staying there. We saw her many times. But we never saw him."

Discouraged but not ready to give up, Yout started to check local police records for his man. Scouring the computers of the Miami Police Department and Metropolitan Police, he came up with a Rory O'Dare arrested for possession of cocaine in the early seventies.

"Well, that looked good," Yout recalled. "The address didn't check out. The description could fit him, but there was no picture in the file and no one knew where the picture was. It was intriguing enough to stick with it."

Still pursuing his quarry, Yout turned up the police officer who had made the arrest on the cocaine charge more than ten years previously. The officer found a file that, of course, had been misfiled. It contained a hawk-like picture.

"It was our man," Yout recalled with considerable glee. And that's how Rod was identified as Rory Paul O'Dare of Miami. The case had become a joint RCMP-DEA investigation, with Rod soon established as the mastermind of the operation. But, according to Yout, Rod was obviously not the financier. Although no prosecutions followed, the DEA believes that "there were plenty of wealthy, and maybe in some cases influential, people behind him."

. . .

While the Miami guys were tracking down Rod, I was facing a health crisis. Most members of my family are big people, and we're all too heavy for our own good. I'm six-foot-one and I used to tip the scales at around four hundred pounds. My doctor was always worried about my weight, but no matter what I did, I couldn't seem to take any of it off by dieting. My doctor in Kentville finally gave up on a diet for me and recommended that I have a stomach stapling operation, a procedure that reduces your weight. There is a long waiting list for this type of an operation, and I was on it for nearly two years. Just as my turn was to come up, the doctor decided to take leave from his practice to go back to medical school and specialize. I found a new doctor in Halifax, but I had to go back to square one on the waiting list.

For some reason I gain weight especially in times of stress, and with all the undercover stuff I had enough stress to supply all of Lockeport. One day early in February 1984, I weighed in at 420 pounds, and the doctor hit the alarm button, telling me I was on the brink of a major heart attack. "You have to have that operation or you're going to drop dead," he declared.

There was nothing to do but tell Rod – and the Mounties – about my problem. Then I checked into Victoria General Hospital in Halifax.

The doctors told Elaine that there was an element of risk with this type of operation, but that they expected no complications in my case. An unexpected breathing problem developed, however, and I almost didn't come around. I was scheduled to be in the recovery room for about two hours, but I was in there for twenty-four hours before they managed to correct the problem.

While I was recovering, Chris and the boys at RCMP Yarmouth sent a fruit basket. They didn't sign their real names, of course. Rod, who also avoided real names, sent flowers.

The fruit basket from the Mounties and the flowers from the mob looked nice together.

I was supposed to stay in hospital for a while, but I was worried about the situation at home. I knew that Elaine and my brother-in-law Jim would have a hard time running the business, and I feared that something would go wrong with the undercover operation. After six days I couldn't stand my hospital bed any longer. I called Elaine and said, "Get my clothes. We're going home." And we did.

It wasn't one of my smarter moves. On my first day at home I installed myself at my desk, with its terrific view of the ocean. I savoured the sound of the waves crashing onto the beach in front of our house and took a quick whiff of the salt air. Then it was back to work. I picked up the telephone and had just started to organize a fish deal when, without warning, I doubled over with incredible stomach pains. Elaine called for a doctor and they rushed me to the hospital in Shelburne. My incision had broken open and become infected.

I settled into my hospital bed, looking forward to taking some time to recover properly. But on the next day I had just dozed off when I felt someone shaking me. I opened my eyes with difficulty. The clock showed that it was four in the morning, and Jim was standing over me.

"I hate to tell you this," he said, "but your father has just dropped dead."

My father was only sixty years old. His health had not been good, but I didn't expect him to go. I just lay in my bed half-dazed, staring at the ceiling. When Elaine walked in at break-fast time, I came fully around. I knew we were needed at my mother's.

We buried my father in the cemetery at Oyster Pond Jed-dore, the small community just northeast of Halifax where he had lived most of his life and where I was born. I was sad to see him go. It reminded me of my own mortality. Although my memories of the funeral are hazy, I remember comforting my mother, and Elaine driving me home to Lockeport. The surgery had taken a lot out of me, and I was now beginning to feel the pressure of my double existence. Like any spy I feared making a mistake and being discovered as an undercover agent by the smugglers. I knew these fellows wouldn't just laugh it off – they were deadly serious. As I rested at home I worked out that exactly six months had passed since the gang of smugglers had contacted me and roped me in. It was a heck of a way to spend an anniversary.

I was still feeling groggy when Rod phoned to ask if I could come down to Boston to meet him. "I'd like us to have a talk. I'd like you to check into the Airport Hilton, and I'll meet you there."

I was still weak but I readily agreed, sensing that this was the start of our new relationship. Elaine booked me on a direct flight from Yarmouth to Boston, reserved a room at the Airport Hilton, and packed a change of bandages. Chris Paley and Phil Pitts had recorded the call and met me to pass on their plans.

"We're going to go to Boston, too, ahead of you. And the people from the DEA are going to bug your room and record the meeting. We'll have it all on tape – and we'd like you to wear a recorder as well."

I didn't like the idea of wearing a transmitter, and I told them I wouldn't do it. I didn't trust their technical people to do it right. And I realized by now that Rod was a professional, and I assumed that he was wise to such things as wireless bodypacks.

When I boarded the plane for Boston I still had stitches all the way down my stomach and the incision had not yet fully healed, but I felt a lot better than I had in weeks. It was good to be doing something again, and the prospects of the meeting with Rod – to be recorded by the police – set the old adrenalin flowing. I took the shuttle bus to the Airport Hilton and got established in the bugged room.

A few minutes later Rod knocked on the door. He was clearly pleased to see me, but the hawk-like face surveyed the room keenly. The door to the next room caught his attention, and I could tell by his expression that it spooked him. I was sure he had no idea that the Mounties and the DEA were on the other side of it with their recording devices. At least that's what I told myself as my stomach turned a few somersaults. But I was badly shaken when he spun around and snapped, "Let's get out of here. Let's go for a walk."

I knew if we left the hotel it would be the end of any surveillance – and of any protection for me. I tried to talk him into staying.

I pointed at the bandages on my stomach. "I don't feel too good. Let's stay here and talk."

"No, we're going for a walk," he insisted.

It was almost as if the man had a sixth sense about danger. He pulled me out of the room and we got into an elevator, went down, and walked through the lobby to the street. Then, bang, he opened the door of a taxicab and we jumped in. As we pulled away, we lost both the RCMP and the DEA.

It was my first demonstration of what Billy Yout referred to as the "spooky" side of Rod. As I got to know him better, I was to see it time and again. He was a master at protecting himself against surveillance. I don't think he ever actually spotted anything while he was with me, but he lived with the assumption that someone might be tailing him. Obviously he had trained himself to throw off anyone who might be following him, until it was second nature to him.

On that first occasion, I was startled and, as you can imagine, more than a bit apprehensive. Here I was with the mastermind of a multimillion-dollar drug smuggling ring, heading to an unknown destination in an unfamiliar city. My heart was beating just a little faster than usual, and I had a feeling of tightness around my throat. But I relaxed a little when the taxi stopped in front of a restaurant and we got out.

It was a vegetarian restaurant. Rod, a guy who made his living importing drugs, was a strict vegetarian and very health-conscious. Even in Nova Scotia he never touched meat or even fish. If no other dish of a vegetarian nature was available, he'd always order a salad. And of course he didn't smoke, and drank only occasionally. He was tall and lean, and he looked like he kept himself fit and trim by exercise.

At dinner he relaxed, too, and started to outline in his distinctive Miami-style Southern accent the details of his plans. "The first thing to do is to buy a boat and establish her as a legitimate fishing vessel," he told me. "We've gotta have a routine for her so that no one will take notice of her comings and goings. Once we do that, we can offload stuff onto her out at sea and no one will pay the slightest attention." He added that the vessel should have a Canadian crew and basically fade into the scenery.

"We'll also have to have a place to store the stuff once it's on shore. But I'll tell you more about that later," he said. This left no doubt in my mind that he was looking to establish a permanent pipeline. This was not to be a mere one-shot operation. The million dollars they'd indicated would be for me was beginning to make sense.

Toward the end of the meal he asked me how much money we'd have to spend for a boat and how much I would need to get the whole thing going. I've forgotten my exact answers, but I held to the principle drummed into me by the Mounties: "Get as much money as possible out of the bad guys." I think I said it might cost a couple of hundred thousand dollars to establish a set-up like the one he had in mind.

Rod didn't faint dead away at that. He said we'd get to the details later. He explained that what he had to do now was look for investors, people who wanted a piece of the action. He said he also needed clearance from people higher up in his own organization.

It struck me then that Rod, moccasins and all, was much like any businessman presenting his plans to his banker. I was impressed with Rod's clear planning and his obvious sense of vision. But I was also shocked that the drug business seemed to be so matter-of-fact, as if we were importing tulip bulbs or, for that matter, moccasins.

After dinner we went back to the hotel in a taxi. Rod paid

me back for my air ticket and my expenses. Then he vanished into the New England night. And the Mounties could hardly wait to find out what they had missed.

•   •   •

The telephone tap tipped off the RCMP that the smugglers wanted me to get a local crew as well as a boat. This gave the Mounties an idea. They saw it as a chance to give me some back-up by bringing in another undercover agent. They had one in mind, and a few days after Rod and the Montreal group left town after testing *Endeavour*, Chris introduced me to the man, only to find I knew him. I had bought fish from him on many occasions.

I promptly dubbed him Mr X. The name suited him. He was a blustering sort of individual, given to a great deal of boasting about all manner of things. I suppose that's why the Mounties were impressed with him. I wasn't.

When we all met in the Grand Hotel in Yarmouth, Sergeant Brent Crowhurst made it clear that Mr X would be compensated for the time he spent on the case. At that meeting the question of compensation for my RCMP work was raised for the first time. The Mounties had realized by now that I was spending a lot of time on the case and that, as a result, my business was suffering.

I wanted to be reimbursed for whatever it cost me, including any losses to my business, but I was not overly concerned. I had spent more than six months on this adventure, and while it was eating into my time, I was enjoying it in a crazy way, and we all expected that it would end within a month or two. Up to this point I had received small amounts of money from Chris to cover expenses, and Crowhurst asked whether I had been receiving these payments. Crowhurst left the subject with the promise that I would be "duly compensated." That was good enough for me; I knew I could trust the Mounties. After all, I was risking my life, and they knew it. Why would I need a formal agreement in writing? I guess it was part of their verification process.

By now Rod was making regular stops in Shelburne or Yarmouth to see me, stopping over on his journey from Montreal to Miami with the money from the organization's drug sales there. Mr X was now on the scene and I considered introducing him to Rod. But the man bragged so much and was such a loud mouth that I decided to be cautious and keep them apart, at least for now. I was sure that Rod wouldn't like him and that he wouldn't be happy with the choice I had made. But I was under pressure to set up a meeting.

I could see a potential problem, but it took care of itself. After a few weeks Mr X decided that this undercover work was just too dangerous, and he wanted out. The RCMP agreed. This was a great relief and Rod and the boys weren't even aware of his existence. The fact that he wanted out made it easy.

I had learned to handle Rod by now, using an approach that had worked in my business dealings. The trick was not to get pushy or aggressive with him. I always deferred to him and pretended that he was teaching me something. Rather than initiate anything, I'd wait for him to ask a question and then answer him. And I never got too bold with him.

But now push was coming to shove. Rod was starting to really press me to find a boat.

·   ·   ·

A couple of weeks after my first Boston trip the dragger *Mustn't Tell* (a very appropriate name, I thought) came up for tender. Not only was she suitably named but she also met the required specifications. She was sixty-five feet long, had a steel hull, and was only a couple of years old.

When Rod called, I told him about her. He said, "How much?"

"She'll probably go for about four hundred thousand dollars," I estimated.

"We can't afford that," he moaned. "Why don't you put in a bid for hundred and fifty thousand and see what happens?"

I did as he told me. But as I'd expected, it wasn't enough to get the boat.

Rod was somewhere overseas when he called to ask how we did with *Mustn't Tell*. He was very upset when he heard the outcome, and that was because things were starting to come together at the other end. He now called from overseas more frequently. I wasn't able to make out from which country, though I presumed it was from somewhere in Europe.

He was always guarded on the phone, but I got the impression that they had a highly sophisticated order system for getting the drugs into the pipeline. Rod, and others from the organization, would go to the country where the stuff was grown or manufactured and, just like in any other business, put in an order. Then they had to scramble to get the stuff transported and unloaded into North America. I guessed that Rod had placed an order, and it was now urgent to get the pipeline set up.

Then I heard that the *Lady Ann*, the boat the engineer Charlie had liked so much, was coming up for bids. I called Rod at once and told him that fifty to fifty-two thousand dollars would take her.

But again Rod felt the price was too high. "Put in thirty-two or thirty-three thousand," he said. I couldn't believe it.

"If that's what you want to do, that's what we'll do," I said. "But it's not enough to buy the boat."

Boats like the *Lady Ann* were publicly auctioned off by the Fishermen's Loan Board, usually because someone had defaulted on payments. But the board would not automatically release a vessel to the highest bidder if it felt the bid wasn't high enough. The board would then hang on to it and try again.

That's exactly what happened to us. To my great surprise, we were the high bidder. But the board felt it wasn't enough for the *Lady Ann*, and they hung on to the boat.

Rod was very angry when he heard that we had failed. Finally he said, "Just go ahead and do what needs to be done. We want that boat. Do whatever you have to to get it."

I put in a bid for fifty thousand, and we got the *Lady Ann*. Rod was as happy as a clam at high water.

The *Lady Ann* was eighty-three feet long, she had a wide beam and an open stern. Her wheelhouse was up front and, of course, she had a steel hull. She also had a checkered past. She had been built in the States and ended up in Canada when she was seized for smuggling. There were rumours that she had been in trouble in the States even before that episode. Her crew faced charges in Boston and had been scheduled to be tried when the captain killed the mate to stop him from testifying. A short time after she had been seized in Canada, Murray Ossinger, a local man, bought her for use as a fishing trawler. But the government had stopped issuing licences around that time, and poor Ossinger, unable to use his expensive new boat for fishing, lost his life savings. Understandably he was bitter, and his case attracted a lot of attention from local politicians and the media.

For the past two years she had rusted away at the dock. But now I had bought her. To be accurate, though she was registered in my name, she really belonged to Rod's drug smuggling organization.

I renamed her *Lady Sharell*, for my daughters, Sharon and Jewell. After consulting Rod, I made arrangements to have her towed to be refitted in a shipyard at Meteghan on the north coast of Nova Scotia, nearly eighty miles away. But first I had to get my hands on the money to pay for her. When I called Rod, he said he'd let me know where and how to pick up the money.

He got back to me a few days later and told me to go to Boston again and follow exactly the same routine as on my first trip there – check into the Airport Hilton and wait to be contacted.

Boston became a regular pick-up point for money whenever I needed it to pay for various phases of the project. I guess Rod picked Boston because it was conveniently located between Miami and Nova Scotia and had direct flights from Yarmouth, Miami, and Montreal, all of which were on Rod's trade route. The DEA later investigated whether there was any special Boston connection to the drug deal. They didn't find one, and they came to the same conclusion that I did: it was just a convenient place to meet.

I took the now-familiar flight from Yarmouth, looking around, as always, hoping that no acquaintances were on the flight to ask awkward questions. It was May, and although the air was still nippy back home on the South Shore, in Boston it felt like summer. I checked into the Airport Hilton with the usual group of RCMP and DEA people in tow.

It wasn't Rod who contacted me this time. It was a stranger who introduced himself as Cheyenne. The name really suited him. He was a rough and burly man in his forties, a rugged character who was part Indian.

Chris Paley managed to pass me a message saying that the DEA agents were desperate to get a picture of Cheyenne, who was new on the Boston scene. They wanted me to take Cheyenne to the hotel bar, where an agent would have a camera in his briefcase. Chris described to me exactly where Cheyenne should sit so that the undercover photographer could get a good likeness.

I was working out how in heck I could manage it when Cheyenne said "Let's have a drink at the bar" even before I got a chance to mention it.

"I'm not a drinking man, but I'll have a 7-Up and ice," I told him, trying not to appear overeager as I steered him to the appointed spot.

We started talking. He turned out to be a good story-teller and we were relaxing very nicely. As we talked I kept shifting so that Cheyenne would also have to turn. I figured out that this would allow the man with the camera in his briefcase to photograph him from every angle. I kept it up for about half an hour, until Cheyenne put down his glass and said quietly, "I'll go and get you the money."

He must have had it in his car, because he reappeared a short time later in my room with a briefcase that was stuffed with great wads of American dollars. It equalled fifty thousand Canadian, plus a bit more for travel expenses. Cheyenne and I shook hands – no receipts in this business, where funny stuff gets you killed – and he left.

I never did find out exactly who Cheyenne was. Some of the DEA agents told people later that he was involved in the drug trade in Philadelphia and that Rod was his supplier there. Because of that relationship, Rod asked him to put up some of the money for the upcoming Canadian shipment. In other words, old Cheyenne was an investor.

After the meeting, I gave the case full of money to Chris to take across the border. This became a routine whenever I received cash in Boston. The Mounties recorded the serial numbers as part of their evidence-gathering and carried the money back to Canada to prevent any problems I might have with customs. Someone might have started asking questions ("Nothing to declare, eh?") if I were discovered with fifty thousand dollars.

My end of the pick-up operation was successful. But there was one sour note. All my efforts with Cheyenne had gone up in smoke. Something had blocked the camera lens in the undercover photographer's briefcase, and none of the pictures turned out.

• • •

That second Boston trip marked a turning point in the operation. It was clear to me now that I was in too deep to get out, even if I wanted to. I had now accepted the fifty thousand dollars from Cheyenne, and Rod and his Miami mobsters expected me to deliver. If I pulled out now – even if I returned the money – the drug dealers were likely to find out about my double role. Even if they didn't, it would have been too dangerous for them to have me on the loose knowing their identities and their plans.

I was in a similar fix with the RCMP. If I withdrew now, they would have no incentive to do anything to protect me. After all, no crime had been committed up to that point and no arrests had been made. I would have been a sitting duck for the guys with guns from Miami.

So it was crucial that no hitches develop. I knew that if one did, I would have to make sure that it·didn't torpedo the deal, no matter what.

CHAPTER FOUR

The Licence Saga

YOU MAY THINK THAT THE TERM UNDERCOVER OPERATION HAS A fine, romantic, cloak and dagger ring to it. But like most things in life, the reality is different. Sure, there was enough danger for a lifetime, danger that set the adrenalin pumping a little bit more than I liked. But one of the most stressful periods in the whole caper had more to do with bureaucracy than with any daring subterfuge. In the summer of 1984, almost exactly a year after the Montreal fish deal, the whole project was threatening to collapse and leave me in a dangerous limbo – all because we couldn't get a fishing licence!

I had assumed that once I bought a boat for the drug venture, the Mounties would make sure there would be no problem with licensing it to go fishing. Certainly, whenever I mentioned the licence to Chris Paley or Phil Pitts, they said, "That'll be a piece of cake. No problem."

I knew, of course, that a fishing licence is a valuable commodity on Canada's east coast. The government became very stingy with them a few years ago, and anyone who has one hangs on to it like a drowning man. It's almost impossible for a private individual to get a new one, although the big companies seem to manage to get the odd one assigned to them. The government feels that they deserve them because their processing plants employ large numbers of people. It's all very political.

The result is that there's a trade in the licences much like the trade in taxicab permits in large cities. And like any scarce commodity, they are expensive.

I didn't expect that the Mounties would have to pay for a licence. I presumed that they would simply put in a request to the Department of Fisheries and Oceans and get a spanking new one issued. Of course, I knew Murray Ossinger's story – he went bankrupt when he couldn't get a licence. He had mustered every politician and reporter behind him, and he and his wife even wrote to Prime Minister Pierre Trudeau. But despite the storm they raised, the answer from Ottawa was a firm no.

That history was not forgotten by the government's bureaucracy. The Mounties went to Ottawa with their request, but the bureaucrats shivered in their boots when they heard that the licence was for Murray Ossinger's old vessel.

"There's no way in the world we're ever going to issue a licence to that boat," one official told Chris. "It's been a political hot potato for so long."

I hadn't told Rod that there might be a problem with the licence, because I didn't know it myself. And now I was in a jam. If we couldn't get the boat out fishing, Rod's whole plan would collapse and he would be out quite a lot of money. There was the fifty thousand dollars he had paid for the *Lady Sharell*, and the estimate for the refit was thirty thousand dollars – and that was my other problem.

I'd had the *Lady Sharell* towed to the shipyard in Meteghan where the work on her was in progress. And already the charges were running astronomically over the estimate. The repairs were to have taken a month, but now they were stretching to nearly three months. I'd already made another trip to Boston to pick up twenty thousand dollars for the shipyard, this time delivered by Cheyenne's eighteen-year-old son. But it was clear to me that the refit cost would exceed a hundred thousand.

I now knew what J.P. Morgan meant when he said that if you have to ask the price of a yacht, you can't afford it. The *Lady Sharell* was not a yacht, but the price of her refit would sure have done justice to one.

I hadn't discussed the mounting bill with Rod, and I was worried stiff. If I now told him about that and then added the news that there would be no licence either, I really feared his reaction and for my safety. I kept thinking back to that first meeting last fall in the car, when he held his pointed finger like a gun and said, "Bang. You bite the dust."

•   •   •

The town of Shelburne, where my scrapyard was, is at its prettiest in the summer. The harbour area has been refurbished as a tourist attraction to reflect the town's rich history. The home of Micmac Indians, Shelburne County was first settled by French Acadians in the 1600s; they were followed by settlers from New England a century later. But the biggest event in the town's history came during the American Revolution, when refugees loyal to the British Crown swelled the population to ten thousand, making it one of the biggest cities in Canada. Most of the refugees moved on, but the Loyalist period made the biggest impact on Shelburne.

The historic restorations of the period's handsome buildings along Dock Street remind us how shipbuilding and trade flourished here from the reign of King George III to the death of Queen Victoria. The ships built in Shelburne were sturdy and serviceable, but none of them reached the fame of the

53

schooner *Bluenose* that came from Lunenburg County, a few miles to the east.

Although like most locals I took all this for granted and wasted no time on it, I could see that the tourists loved to poke through the old houses, factories, and museums, as well as the reconstructed dory-building shop once owned by John Williams. The dory – a flat-bottomed rowboat that could be stacked neatly on the deck of a fishing schooner and was used to bring fish back to the mother ship – was for a century the most popular small craft in the Atlantic provinces. A tour of the workshop is popular with the summer tourist crowd.

In his casual clothes Rod blended right in with the tourists on his now frequent visits to Shelburne. Our scrapyard was a few blocks from the tourist area and not as pretty. But then Rod didn't come to see the sights. He'd never stay very long – a few days at the most – and he'd check into either the Oxbow Motel on Shelburne's outskirts or at Rodd's Grand Hotel in Yarmouth. I'd pick him up at the airport in Yarmouth or Halifax, drive him around in my half-ton, and then drop him off again when it was time for him to leave.

We'd got to the shipyard in Meteghan to see the *Lady Sharell*, and he'd inspected the progress of the refit. He wanted her equipped with the latest radar and electronic equipment, and he decided to buy it in the States and ship it to Nova Scotia. It all seemed routine. He knew exactly what equipment was needed and where to get it. He ordered navigation gear, radar, and a radio set. I'd pick it up at Yarmouth airport and take it to the shipyard in Meteghan. We'd pay the full duty on it, and it was all perfectly legal.

Nevertheless, an electronics firm in Yarmouth had heard about the shipments and went to the RCMP to complain that the gear was being brought in without the customs duty being paid. The RCMP branch responsible for that end of things investigated and found everything legal. I laughed when Chris told me about it, but it was a warning to me that we were attracting attention among the locals.

Chris and Phil were also aware of all the local buzz about

my activities, and they were anxious not to have the case wrecked by some local busybody. "We'd like you to lease a half-ton, one that would fade better into the scenery here than the one you're driving," Chris said one day. I'd been playing chauffeur to Rod in my trusty old Chevy half-ton, which had "Shelburne Scrap and Metal" emblazoned on its sides. I thought it didn't stick out all that much from other pickups on the South Shore, but the Mounties were afraid that people would remember the firm's name in strange locations and maybe even associate Rod with it. I followed their instructions and leased a spanking new truck from Avis in Yarmouth. The Mounties had another trick up their sleeve: they installed a tape recorder under the dashboard. My conversations with Rod were to be immortalized on tape.

I must admit that the recorder worried me, and over the next few months I would have many an anxious moment over it. One day I was driving with Rod and noticed that he kept staring at the exact place in the dashboard where the recorder was hidden. He just stared, hawk-like, not saying a word. Soon I was sweating profusely, convinced that with that spooky sixth sense of his he had noticed something. But it was a false alarm. He was just daydreaming. Another time some of his Miami people came up to Nova Scotia and they borrowed my truck before I could say no, and my heart was stuck in my throat until they returned. I was afraid that they might for some reason look under the dashboard and find the recorder. Again, luck was on my side, and they didn't notice a thing.

My relationship with Rod was growing chummy by now. I still let him do all the talking and tried to give the impression that I was in awe of him. I could see that the technique was working and that he had complete confidence in me. But his inbred caution about being followed carried over into his conversation, and he never really told me more than I needed to know. The impression I had of him was that of a cool professional.

But once he exposed a reckless side that confirmed my

suspicion that there were other dimensions to Rod. He always told me that he never used drugs himself, and I had no reason to doubt him. I knew he was a strict vegetarian and that he was health-conscious in the extreme, so I assumed that he would never use drugs.

On one of his visits he took a very long time to get out of the arrival area at Yarmouth airport. I was waiting to pick him up, and when he finally came out I had a feeling that something had gone wrong. But he said nothing while I drove him to the Oxbow Motel. A day or two later, after we'd made our customary rounds of the shipyard, we stopped off at Shelburne Scrap and Metal to cool off. We were inside the office sipping on soft drinks when he suddenly said, "I did something very stupid. I brought a bit of coke with me and the customs people found it in my bag."

It was a small amount, not enough to lay charges. The customs people confiscated it and gave him a warning. But it shook him up.

"I swear, I'll never do that again," he told me. "I don't want to do anything to jeopardize our operation."

Chris confirmed the story later, and I was amazed to see this unprofessional side to Rod. For all their superb organization, the drug smugglers, too, were subject to human weaknesses.

•   •   •

In a way I was pleased that Rod had made a mistake. I felt that I might need his understanding for a few foibles of my own. The two problems that threatened to scuttle the project were still hanging over me. I hadn't found a way to get a fishing licence, and I still had not told Rod that the cost of the *Lady Sharell*'s refit had more than tripled from its original estimate. I was getting near desperation and losing a lot of sleep. To clear my head I used to drive to the shipyard in Meteghan to watch the refit.

One day I was again driving to Meteghan when on an impulse I pulled into my old friend Ken Sweeney's fish plant just to chat. I was hungry for some small talk not connected with the case, but I guess the licence was very much on my mind because I started to tell him my problems. He knew, of course, like everyone else in the area, that I had bought the *Lady Sharell*. Many pairs of eyes were watching closely to see whether I would get the licence that Murray Ossinger didn't.

"I don't know what I'm going to do," I told Ken. "They're not issuing any more licences. You just can't get them any more."

He looked at me and said, "I've got a licence I could sell you."

I couldn't believe my ears as he went on: "My father had a vessel that sank and he took its licence and put it on an old, derelict boat just to hold on to it. We've still got the old boat and the licence. If there's any way that you could revive the licence, okay, I'll sell it to you."

I wasn't sure whether the licence could be transferred, but it was the only hope I had at this point. So we quickly agreed that I would pay twenty-five thousand dollars if the licence could be shifted to the *Lady Sharell*, and I drove directly to see Cliff Hood, a lawyer who had done some work for me in the past.

"Cliff, we've got to get this licence," I told him as soon as I sat down in his office. Of course I didn't tell him why. But my urgent tone caught his attention, and he promised to start work on it right away. He did move quickly, and within a week he arranged for the licence to be transferred.

I was delighted. I phoned Chris right away and told him that we had a licence. He told Phil Pitts and the other Mounties, and they all thought it was a miracle. That, by the way, was also Elaine's reaction. She is convinced to this day that it was divine intervention.

But I still had one more hurdle to jump. I assumed that the RCMP would come up with the twenty-five thousand dollars to pay Ken Sweeney for the licence. Chris and Phil didn't think it would be a problem. "We'll look after it," they said.

But a few days later they returned with a message of gloom and doom.

"We can't get it through." They said they had talked to their superiors and the word had come down from Halifax or Ottawa that no money was to be provided.

I couldn't believe it. It didn't make any sense. We had all put a lot of effort into this investigation, not to mention the risks I had taken. Now it was in danger of falling to pieces – and the pieces would probably fall on me. The Mounties in Yarmouth seemed to me as straight as a loon's leg, and they made no secret of their disgust with the higher ranks of the force. I don't know to this day what the reasoning was for refusing the money. I do know that they had a strict rule to use the smugglers' money whenever possible. Fair enough. But I couldn't do it in this case. I had never told Rod that the fishing licence would cost money. He was going to be upset enough about the refit expenses – when I got around to telling him. The only explanation I could think of was that the RCMP brass were afraid that if it came out that they had paid for the licence, they'd be caught in the middle of the Murray Ossinger affair.

I didn't have much time to brood about it. I knew that for me there was no choice. Whether the RCMP brass liked it or not, I had to come up with the money. I don't want to get too dramatic, but I felt it was a matter of life and death. I didn't want to have to face Rod to explain that I had forgotten to mention such an important detail. With the amount of money tied up in the venture now, I didn't think I would get away without being harmed.

I did the only thing I could. I phoned my banker, Bill Sharpe, in Shelburne and made an appointment with him.

"Can I get a loan of twenty-five thousand dollars?" I asked. "I'm prepared to take out a mortgage on our home."

"That's fine," he said. "But we'll have to have the mortgage as a collateral."

Once again, he asked no further questions. He was used to me by now. There was no risk to the bank in any case. They had our home as security. I was getting into this thing deeper and deeper.

Finally I decided that I couldn't put off any longer telling Rod about the refit bill.

"How much is this going to cost us?" he fumed at me on the phone, cussing a blue streak. "This is way out of line. You better let me see all the bills."

I knew by now that huge amounts of money were involved in drug smuggling. But the operation was run just like any other business. Organizers, even masterminds like Rod, had to watch their expenses and to make sure that subordinates didn't direct the money into their own pockets. Clearly, Rod had to go higher up in his organization to explain why more cash was needed.

When he called a few days later he was much calmer. He asked me to meet him in Montreal to pick up the money that I needed. I was to look after the hotel reservations. I reported the scheduled meeting to Chris and Phil, and they decided that once again the RCMP should bug my room so that they would have on tape whatever Rod ended up saying.

The RCMP picked the hotel, one of the big modern ones right downtown. I flew to Montreal, checked into the hotel, and turned on the TV while waiting for Rod. A few minutes later Chris Paley knocked on the door and stuck his head in to tell me to turn the TV down, then to give me a peek at their recording set-up next door. A woman RCMP officer, with headphones, was doing the recording, while Chris and Phil were set to listen. I scurried back to my room and settled down to watch the now turned-down TV set.

It wasn't long before Rod knocked at the door. He was carrying a brown briefcase. He sat down and slowly went over all the bills I had brought. In the end he seemed satisfied and relaxed a little.

Then he reached for his briefcase and said, "Here's seventy grand. I haven't counted it."

I took a look and saw the money was all in small bills, fives, tens, and some twenties. "No problem," I said.

I kept Rod talking. I'd been instructed to make conversation so the Mounties next door could get as many details on tape as possible. So I rambled on about how this was going to be the final refit bill.

This time Rod didn't suspect anything. Once again there was an adjoining door to the next room, where the RCMP listening post was, but for some reason it didn't bother him. We kept on talking for some time, mostly about the cost of boat refits, and again he said, "It'll all come together soon." But his sixth sense must have set off a buzzer in his head because out of the blue he said, "Come on, we're going out for dinner."

"Where are we going?" I asked, ever conscious of our Mountie eavesdroppers. If he said the name of a place, they could try to cover it with someone.

"We'll go downstairs somewhere," he replied.

"What about the money?"

"We'll leave it here," he replied without hesitation.

So we left the seventy thousand in cash sitting in a briefcase on the carpet next to a dresser. This was another demonstration of the reckless side to Rod.

We went out of the room, got on the elevator, and he pressed the button to go down a couple of floors. Then he quickly pressed the button to go up. We went to the top floor, to the hotel's very elegant roof restaurant, while the Mounties scurried around the downstairs lobby, looking for us everywhere. They found us after a while; I spotted Chris dashing down the hallway leading to the restaurant. But there was nothing they could do to resume recording our conversation. Rod was very good at this kind of game. Again, I don't think he suspected a thing. He just acted this way out of habit.

At dinner, as usual, Rod ordered a large salad and some fruit. We had a great many meals together, and not once did I see him deviate from his vegetarian habit. We enjoyed the night-time view of the city, and Rod went to great lengths to stroke me for the good job I had done.

"The boat is going to be okay. When you phoned the other

day I was startled at how much we would need. Don't forget, there are other people in on this, and they want to see where their money goes. We'll get everything organized and get our money back," he said. Like a good manager or a good salesman he wanted to reassure me after his explosion of anger on the phone. Seeing all the bills had convinced him that the expenses were genuine, and I'm sure he chalked up the overrun to my inexperience.

Our conversations never touched on anything personal. But on this evening he let drop that he grew up in Miami in a working-class neighbourhood and that he now could afford a lovely house in a rich area. He was an avid sailor and glowingly described his sailboat.

"You'll have to come down and see how I live," he said, but didn't mention any specific date. I had a feeling that his life on the road was boring and lonely. I couldn't have been a terribly amusing companion for him, though he could at least relax with me as opposed to dining with a total stranger. I guess in the normal course of events in the drug trade you had to be careful all the time. You never knew when your trail might be picked up.

.   .   .

The next day I flew home, with the Mounties carrying the seventy thousand dollars inside the brown brief-case Rod had left me. When I got home, I asked Elaine to take the case to the bank in Shelburne. It hadn't occurred to me that such an amount in small bills might cause problems, but Elaine instantly realized that she couldn't just go up to the teller with the money without setting the whole town talking.

There was already enough gossip about us in town. Eyebrows were raised when I bought the *Lady Sharell*, and the local observers had a real field day when I got the fishing licence. Small bills for such a large amount of money would have set the town abuzz even more. It might have even spelled "drug deal" to some people. That is why Elaine decided to be cautious. The teller system is so public and, as she said, "you never know who's in line behind you."

She went to Bill Sharpe's office, knocked on the door, and asked him to take the deposit there rather than at the counter. Bill Sharpe instantly got three tellers together and with their help counted the money in his office.

"I had a hard time to keep from smiling," Elaine told me when she got home. "I just knew something was going on in their minds as they were counting all these tens and twenties, and I was wondering what it was."

Bill Sharpe never asked where the money came from, and I've never asked what he thought at the time. Just another customer depositing seventy thousand dollars in small bills, I guess.

• • •

With the *Lady Sharell*'s refit almost completed, Rod was pressuring me to find a captain. Every time I saw him or talked to him on the phone he'd say, "Let's get the show on the road. We've got to get her fishing, we've got to get her established. We need a skipper."

That was Rod's plan – a legitimate fishing trawler with a legitimate Canadian crew fishing just like all the other boats. Every once in a while it would pick up a cargo of drugs for him, and no one would be the wiser. The RCMP and I had some problems with that. The Mounties didn't want to involve a Canadian crew, and neither did I. If I hired a crew and its members took part in the smuggling scheme, I would have enticed them into a crime they might otherwise not have committed. But if they were told that I was undercover for the RCMP, word was bound to spread like wildfire, and I would have to fear for my safety. To avoid entrapping some locals, the best bet was to persuade Rod to use a crew from the United States. But Rod resisted the suggestion. So when it became urgent to have the boat start fishing, I decided to hire a local skipper, with the idea of pulling him out before the drug deal was to take place.

I was lucky enough to be able to hire an excellent local skipper, Gordon Hollett. As it happened, Hollett had unique qualifications to command the *Lady Sharell*. He had been her skipper when Murray Ossinger owned her, and he had taken her to sea in preparation for Murray's fishing venture. But when Murray didn't get his licence, Hollett became the skipper of another boat.

Hollett was a high-line fisherman, which in local terms means he was as good a man as you could get, the finest kind of skipper. He had come to see me at the scrapyard while the *Lady Sharell* was still on the slip at Meteghan and told me, "If you're looking for someone to take her, I'm your man. I think I can do a good job for you." Now I told him: "Gordon, you take the boat." He hired a crew, and they started doing up her gear – rigging her for swordfishing – to start on the first day of September.

Rod came up to meet Hollett, and he liked him instantly. Hollett, a man of few words, exuded an air of quiet confidence and was a typical low-key Maritimer. Nothing was said about the drug deal. I assume that Rod, who believed that everyone was greedy and wanted to make money no matter how, expected Hollett to join the venture readily when the time came. I knew that Hollett was a straightshooter, and I started praying that I would find a way to extricate him before the drug shipment came.

The fishing venture was plagued by bad luck from the very beginning. On Hollett's first night out at sea, a giant wave swept the wheelhouse and took out one of its windows. The glass shattered, barely missing the wheelman. The wave destroyed some of the electronics, and she had to limp back into Shelburne while workmen from the Meteghan shipyard came and fixed the damage. Hollett took her back out after swordfish and kept her out through the big tides of September and October. But the catch was meagre, even after he changed her gear for halibut fishing. It was not a good season for fish, and we never made enough money to pay for the gear.

Hollett took a Christmas break and went out again in January, fishing her hard on the Grand Banks off Newfoundland in really bad winter weather. Fishing in the North Atlantic is always tough on boats as well as the crews, and despite her expensive refit, the *Lady Sharell* was developing major mechanical trouble. Her entire keel began to vibrate, and a quick inspection showed that the problem was the shaft. She needed a new shaft. And there were other problems. I could hardly believe it. Nor could Rod.

"Do whatever it takes. I want her fixed and fixed right," he told me grimly. He said he'd buy a new shaft himself in the States and ship it up to me. Since the damage was not life-threatening, I sent her back out for a couple more trips, hoping to recover some of my costs. At the same time, I made arrangements with a shipyard in Liverpool for another major refit to start once the shaft arrived.

"She's got to be ready to go within a month," Rod stressed. "We'll pay whatever it takes." He also announced that he would send up his own man, an expert, to supervise the refit.

I didn't know how that would unfold, but the refit solved one major problem for me. I now had an excuse to remove Gordon Hollett from the enterprise. Since the boat was going to be laid up for a while, I told Hollett that he and the crew better look for another job.

He was disappointed, but he saw my point, and we parted on friendly terms.

CHAPTER FIVE

Life on the Home Front

AS YOU'D IMAGINE, MY DOUBLE LIFE WAS BECOMING MORE DIFFI-
cult every day. Not only did I have to play-act with Rod but
my family didn't know what I was doing. Elaine did, of course.
But Sharon and Jewell didn't and neither did Elaine's extended
clan, who were all around us.

The kids were used to my dashing about the South Shore
doing business at all times of day and night. But children –
even though they may be teenagers – quickly pick up on

anything unusual. And they sensed the tension. They didn't ask me any questions, but I knew they were aware that something was going on. There were strange phone calls at strange hours, and the girls caught Elaine and me whispering on several occasions. Also, I guess, the strain showed on my face.

Later I found out that Sharon told Elaine's sister, Gayla, only half in jest: "I don't know what's going on. I think Dad is dealing in drugs."

Elaine knew of my activities in great detail because it was very important for me to have someone to share my double life with, and she proved to be a tower of strength. I don't think I would have gotten all the way through the operation without her.

Actually, we succeeded in keeping the kids out of it for quite a long time. It was not until the end of 1984 that Sharon, sixteen at the time, began to suspect that something was seriously wrong. That year we took a Christmas holiday in Daytona Beach, Florida (far away from Miami), and it was one of the best vacations I ever had. We just went swimming and lay on the beach day after day. I managed to unwind totally, and that was the tipoff to Sharon. She immediately picked up on the difference in my mood and realized that I was under a lot of pressure back home.

Later she recalled: "After we came back from vacation after the turn of the year, it was back to the old grind. I remember thinking something was going on because he was gone constantly. He was gone a lot anyway – he's a very up-and-at-'em type. But now he was gone all the time. And I wasn't allowed to go with him anymore. Usually, when he went away before, I'd go with him when I was home from school. We were really close. I remember saying, 'Dad, I want to go with you,' and he'd say, joking, 'Well no, because I'm not sure when I'm coming back.' I know now that he was going to see the drug smugglers, or the Mounties."

My meetings with the Mounties took place in true spy-story fashion. We had three or four prearranged places where we could meet unobserved. The one we used most frequently was the entrance to an old ammunition storage dump on a disused Defence Department range on the Sandy Point Road outside Shelburne. We'd refer to it as the "first place" on the phone when arranging to meet.

The entrance to the storage dump was flanked by a rising concrete wall, like a tunnel without a roof. The place, and the approach to it, was overgrown, so it was easy to park a couple of vehicles there without being observed. I used to drive the Avis pickup nose-first into the entrance, and Chris and Phil would change the tapes in the hidden recorder. (I never did get to hear what they sounded like.) Then we'd sit in the undercover car, and the Mounties would write down in their notebooks whatever I had to report about Rod's activities.

A few weeks after our return from Florida, I had a startling new development to report to Chris and Phil. Rod had asked me to buy a property, a secluded house or a farm where we could store his shipments once they reached shore. This stash site, as he called it, would serve as a warehouse until the stuff was shipped to suppliers in Montreal or Toronto. Chris and Phil were not surprised, telling me it was all part of a pattern, and after they consulted with people up the line, they gave me very specific instructions: "We don't want you putting this property or any other in your name. If they want to buy real estate, let them do it under their own names."

Perhaps they didn't want me getting in too deeply, and it might have smacked of entrapment. Anyway, I was just as happy not to have to buy property, and I also had the perfect excuse to use on Rod.

"It's not a good idea for me to own the place," I told him. "There's already a lot of talk in town about where I got the money to buy the *Lady Sharell* and how I managed to get the fishing licence. Buying a property would draw even more attention to me, and I don't think we want that."

The hawk-like face hardened, then relaxed. "Okay, that

makes sense," he conceded. "But keep your eyes open for a place that might do. It has to be secluded – no close neighbours – but accessible."

Rod not only wanted no neighbours but he wanted a place that was set back from the main road and, if possible, on the water. The drug smuggling business had specs for boats, and now I discovered that they also had an exact plan for stash sites. Clearly this operation was not to be a single shipment, but the start of a permanent pipeline into North America through this little corner of Nova Scotia.

Sharon was clearly bothered by all the strange happenings, which was quite at odds with Jewell's easygoing acceptance of it all. She used to plague Elaine with a stream of questions, and Elaine couldn't give her sensible answers. One day, when the questions were particularly probing, Elaine said: "Sharon, you've got to stop asking all these questions. It's really a matter of life and death."

Sharon now somewhat sheepishly admits that she rushed right over to her aunt Gayla and told her what her mother had said.

"I just didn't think at all," she said recently. "I did take it in, but I couldn't understand whose life and death. It didn't make much sense."

I don't know what Gayla made of it all, but she kept her counsel.

Life at home was not without its lighter moments. The girls got to know Chris Paley well but not his true role, thanks to Elaine's clever idea for a cover story. He had occasion to phone so often that Elaine thought it would be wise if we had some sort of an explanation for his frequent phone calls. So we told the girls he was an associate of mine, just starting in the fish business.

But soon Chris played a larger part in the girls' lives. He was a keen hockey player and was a prominent member of the Yarmouth hockey team. One day he asked us to go to see him play in Shelburne, and the whole family went. The kids enjoyed it, and before long the trip to Shelburne became a regular family expedition. The games were once a week and they were lots of fun. We didn't know anybody on the Shelburne team, so we rooted for Yarmouth.

Chris was just a young fellow – around thirty – and he made an impression on Sharon and Jewell. To tell you the truth, Elaine thinks they had a bit of a crush on him. They used to call him Papa Smurf, and Elaine encouraged the nickname because she worried that someone might wonder about it if they cheered for him by his real name. He had served a tour of duty in Yarmouth once before and was pretty well known in town as an RCMP officer.

The girls were so taken with him that they even took some of their friends from school to the games and told them, "This is a friend of Dad's, that Chris fellow. Watch him play. He's really good."

In one game toward the end of the season, Chris played really well. The next day the RCMP announced that he was being transferred from Yarmouth (although he was going to stay on my case). The local radio sportscaster must have received a press release about it, because the next morning, when he described how well Yarmouth had done the previous night in the game with Shelburne, he added that he was sorry to hear Yarmouth was about to lose its best player.

"Chris Paley will be leaving. His employer" – Jewell and Sharon were getting ready for school in the next room, and Elaine lunged to turn down the radio really fast – "the RCMP of Yarmouth, is moving him elsewhere." Elaine worried that they might have heard the newscast. "That's all we need is for them to go to school and say, 'Guess what? My Dad's friend is really an RCMP guy.'" But we heard no more about it.

Elaine was very close to Gayla and her other sister in Lockeport, Betty. They saw each other or talked on the phone at least once a day. Elaine often babysat their children, and she used to say that Betty's daughter, Brandys, was almost her own, since she practically grew up at our house. Betty's husband, Bob, was away fishing a lot, and at those times Betty and Brandys would stay with us. Brandys is a bright and lovable, free-hearted child, a real joy to have around.

On Sundays and sometimes on other days we would all go out together for lunch at the Loyalist Inn in Shelburne. We'd sit and gossip and discuss family things, and, as you'd expect, everybody knew everyone else's business in great detail.

Now, all of a sudden, there was a whole area of our life that we couldn't discuss with anybody because it was too dangerous. Slip-ups were always a real possibility, and the fewer people who knew – even in the family – the better.

Not only could Elaine not tell her sisters but she had to be on guard all the time about what she said. All she had to do was to drop a phrase like, "I was talking about that to Chris Paley the other day," and her sisters would have immediately demanded to know who Chris Paley was. Or she might have mentioned, "Leonard is in Boston again," and that, too, would have piqued their curiosity.

So although we hated to do it, we cut back on our contacts with them. Not completely, but the relationship became strained.

The danger of being discovered was constant. Once Betty walked in during one of Elaine's frequent phone calls with Chris Paley. "She soon realized that I was being careful of what I was saying, so she went to the basement family room and visited with Sharon and Jewell until I got off the phone."

At that point Elaine didn't mention what the conversation was and Betty didn't ask. She told Elaine later that she realized something was going on, but trusted that we would tell her when it was time for her to know. Gayla, too, never once mentioned all of Sharon's outpourings about what was going on in our house. I suppose, like Betty, she was waiting to be told at the appropriate time what was making us act so strangely.

•   •   •

With all the secret meetings in Boston or at the shipyard with Rod, and then the even more secret meetings with the Mounties, I was neglecting the scrapyard and the fish business. My partner, Jim Dooks, bore the brunt of my enforced absence. Jim is a heavy-set bear of a man with a beard but less hair on top than he once had, and is a good-natured person with a great sense of humour and a lot of patience. He put up with my strange behaviour for a few months. But when my appearances at the scrapyard became less and less frequent, one day he blew up at me in the office.

"You're not keeping up your end of the business," he yelled at me. "We have an agreement that you handle the selling and the wheeling and dealing, and you're not doing it. You're running around doing the Lord knows what, while I'm trying to run the yard and the sales, too, and it's not working."

Jim was well within his rights to complain. Our working arrangement was exactly as he described it. That's how we had set it up when he joined me in the business right out of the Canadian Armed Forces, where he had been a corporal in the Service Corps and had been posted around the world to places like Germany and the Gaza Strip, where his unit was part of the United Nations contingent. Jim and Elaine were very close, and when I saw signs that he and his wife, Carol, were getting tired of military life, I suggested to him that he become a partner in Shelburne Scrap and Metal.

Sure enough, Jim took out his army pension contributions, invested the money in the business, and proved to be a devoted and hard worker. He'd work through the night if necessary and never complain. But he was no businessman. With me devoting so much time to the undercover work, he had to deal with the business end in addition to his usual chores, and it was simply too much for him.

Elaine, who did some of the office work, could see money being lost and deals going down the drain because, as she said, "Leonard wasn't there to make the decision and to handle it. For example, we'd buy fish from someone and leave the shipment for somebody to handle locally. If Leonard were around, he'd make sure it moved out fast. But if no one prodded the handlers, the shipment would sit for two or three days and we'd lose thousands of dollars. One time we were supposed to buy fish from a guy and then we found out the fish was no good, so we cancelled the deal. But then the man phoned and told Jim, 'I'd already bought it and you have to go in for half of it.' Jim just couldn't deal with that, so I had to write a cheque for maybe thirty-five hundred dollars. If Leonard had been there, things sure wouldn't have happened that way.

"Jim couldn't get the same price for scrap metal that Leonard would get, even though they sold it to the same person all the time. With Jim he'd say he'd pay a certain price, but when the cheque came it was for less. Leonard would get on the phone and say, 'Hey, bucky, you promised us a certain price, you send the cheque or I'll be there to pick it up.' And he would get it. But Jim would say, 'If you could do that, that will be fine but if not, whatever you can do.' That's the type of person he is."

There was no doubt I was the businessman. But this businessman was being an undercover agent and was rarely around.

My neglect went on from the time we bought the *Lady Sharell* in May 1984 until the operation ended a year later. As you'd imagine, I didn't like the situation any more than Jim or Elaine did. We couldn't defend my conduct to Jim without revealing what I was up to, which would endanger him, too. I knew I had to find a way to keep Jim off my back until the ordeal was over. So after our quarrel I tried a new tack.

"I may sell the business, Jim," I told him with a weary shake of the head. There had, in fact, been someone around asking whether I was interested in selling the scrapyard, and I knew I might want to sell once the operation ended, especially if I had to relocate. But I also knew that Jim wouldn't want me to sell. That would keep him from pushing the quarrel too far, and I would win some badly needed time. I was sure that once Jim found out what I had been up to, I'd have his full support. But what I needed for the moment was to have him on my side without telling him.

We talked about selling the business for several days, and

Jim finally said, "I don't want you to sell. I make my living here and so do you. So let's make the best of it."

I felt like a rat. But I knew I had won. I promised Jim that I'd try to do the job as we had agreed and put more hours into the yard. I was pretty sure I couldn't keep that promise, but it would quiet down Jim for a while.

• • •

We also had to cut back our contacts with other people in town. Elaine and I reluctantly agreed that it would be too easy to make a dangerous slip if we kept up our regular flow of visitors. It was easier to shy away from people altogether. We even stopped going to church for about three months, which led to a number of incidents that in retrospect are funny, but were not funny at the time.

Elaine had taught Sunday school in Lockeport for years and years to a class of nine- to eleven-year-old girls. They used to do a lot of things together, and she enjoyed it immensely. When the possibility came up that we might have to leave, Elaine decided to resign well before the end of the term so that the church would have lots of time to get a replacement. She phoned her friend Lorna, who was in charge of the Sunday school program, and Lorna was absolutely shocked. She proceeded to give Elaine such a sharp lecture about being dependable and being faithful that Elaine phoned Chris Paley right away to complain that she had just received the worst tongue-lashing of her life and that she couldn't say a single thing in response.

Our absence from church provoked a visit from our minister, the Reverend Bob Burke. He couldn't understand why we weren't coming, since we had been members of his Pentecostal congregation for years and had attended the Sunday services regularly. Elaine was at home when he called, and she came up with a reason that contained a grain of truth.

"We've got problems with some of the people in the congregation," she told him. "They're giving us a hard time because of the boat and the licence. There's a lot of jealousy, and Leonard and I are finding it hard to take. I think we'll stay away for a while."

Burke stared at her wide-eyed, and then, like Lorna the Sunday school supervisor, he gave her a stern lecture, this one about the need to be more merciful. Elaine didn't respond, taking comfort in the knowledge that he, like Lorna, would approve once he found out the true story.

The reasons Elaine gave were not too far off the truth. When we stopped socializing with people in town, stories went around that we had our noses up in the air because of our sudden success. It must have seemed that way, but it wasn't true. We didn't like breaking off our social life, but there was no other way.

Lockeport is only a small place. The town's official sheet, which they hand out to visitors at the Little School Museum – Lockeport's Centennial Year project – says the population is "approximately 929." But I doubt whether the community numbers much more than seven hundred these days. One thing is certain, though: it's small enough for everyone to know everyone else's business. That means you can't get involved in something like an undercover operation and not have people notice that something is in the wind.

My next-door neighbour would see my truck rolling in at twelve o'clock at night or even during the early morning hours. He'd certainly take notice. Nothing was ever said to me, but I could sense eyebrows going up all over town, and I could just hear the whispers of "Mitchell is up to something."

As in all small towns, Lockeport has the usual share of petty jealousies. That meant that the "something" I was up to would have to be illicit or illegal. After all, what goes on after dark? Many of the locals thought I was into smuggling, or having an affair with another woman. Or perhaps both.

Before the mob dropped into my life, our lifestyle had been pretty constant and not a really high-spending one. Now, all of a sudden I had bought a boat. Since she was purchased from the Loan Board, everyone who cared could find out how much I had paid for her. And now she was being refitted, obviously at considerable expense, in Meteghan. There was a lot of speculation about where I got the money.

Then I got a fishing licence, and the boat went swordfishing. At that, word travelled like wildfire along the South Shore because everyone knew that Murray Ossinger had faced ruin because he couldn't get a licence for the same boat. The news media knew the story, too, and reporters from the CBC in Halifax came chasing after me even before I had the licence. They suspected that I had some sort of deal worked out to get a licence. If they only knew the truth! But of course I couldn't tell them about the contortions I had to go through to get the licence.

One day a very persistent reporter wanted to know what I'd do with the *Lady Sharell* if I didn't get a licence.

"I'll cut her up for scrap," I replied. The startling answer washed, and for a while the questions stopped. But before long the reporters were back at it. They even went to the shipyard in Meteghan where the *Lady Sharell* was being re-fitted, asking a lot of questions and taking pictures of the boat.

The old line "any publicity is good publicity" doesn't apply to the drug smuggling business. The last thing I wanted was for Rod to read somewhere that the *Lady Sharell* was a hot political potato and that there was trouble over the fishing permit. Somewhat naively, I guess, I expected the RCMP to control the publicity. I know it was irrational, and later, when I needed the media myself, I was glad that I lived in a country where the police *don't* control what's published.

CHAPTER SIX

The Gentleman Smuggler

THE MAN ROD SENT TO SUPERVISE THE SECOND REFIT TURNED OUT to be a qualified captain and salvage expert named Ed Knight. Like Rod, Ed was from south Florida. I met him for the first time a day or so after he arrived and checked into the Privateer Inn in Liverpool, some thirty miles north of Lockeport. The scene sticks in my mind because he and Rod were such a contrast. Here was Rod towering over Ed by what looked like a couple of feet and looking lean and mean. Rod was wound up most of the time, ready to pounce like a hawk. Ed, a distinguished-looking man in his early fifties, clean-shaven and with dyed brown hair, seemed much more relaxed and suave, even in casual clothes.

He was a bit reserved as Rod introduced us, taking my

measure, as I was taking his. We made a few casual remarks about boats and fishing, and I sensed right away that he was a man of the sea and that he must have been a fisherman at one time just like me. Soon he was asking to see the boat, obviously anxious to get on with his assigned task.

"She's still out fishing, but she should be back in within a day or so," I said.

We had a pleasant lunch at the Privateer Inn's wood-panelled dining room. The restaurant was famous for its seafood. But Rod, true to form, ordered a large salad. I think Ed, it turned out, also ate mostly vegetarian fare, but he would on occasion eat fish. It seems crazy looking back on it, but the drug mob from Florida that I was to meet during this venture were all very health-conscious. They kept in shape by jogging, and they watched what they ate. I guess it was part of a wider trend toward health-consciousness. I didn't complain because it all helped increase the demand for fish around the world and so kept the price up.

Over lunch Rod explained that Ed would not only supervise the refit but that he would also be captain of the *Lady Sharell* after her repairs were completed. So Ed would be the one to take her out on the drug run.

"Ed has a lot of experience," Rod said. "But I'd still like you to find a Canadian crew. That'll make it all seem normal."

I didn't say much in response, but I knew it would be a foggy Friday before I rounded up a Canadian crew. No way. I had to think of how to talk Rod into flying a crew from the United States. For now, I decided to bide my time and wait for an opportunity to scuttle the idea of a local crew.

A day or two after our lunch, Gordon Hollett brought the *Lady Sharell* into Shelburne with her catch on board. He had her unload, then brought her around to the Government Wharf at Lockeport.

I drove Ed to Lockeport where he got his first look at his new ship. He got on board for the trip to the shipyard in Liverpool, and I hopped in my half-ton and drove to meet them there.

Ed was shocked by the boat's condition. In his words, she was ruined. He said she was vibrating badly, one of the bearings was severely out of alignment, and the bottom of her keel had a crack in it. We faced a major repair, there was no doubt about that. When I told Hollett about it, he realized that she would probably be on the slip for the rest of the fishing season. So he just said calmly, "Well, it's better if I go." Luckily he and the crew soon got another boat and went out to fish again.

Meanwhile, Ed had ordered a rewelding job and arranged for struts to be put in along with a new shaft. Rod went off to the States to buy the shaft and send it up. Eventually the *Lady Sharell* would be repaired, but Ed was never completely happy with her.

With the boat up on the slip, I now went to see Ed almost every day. We'd have lunch at various places but mostly at the Privateer Inn. The inn's name was appropriate for the location of our illegal discussions, but really refers to the days when Liverpool was the privateering capital of Nova Scotia. During the American Revolution, His Majesty's Yankees (the term used as a title by Liverpool's famous author Thomas Raddall) were torn between ties of kinship to New England cousins and their ties as loyal British subjects. Eventually Yankee raids caused the Liverpool skippers to take sides. They obtained "letters of marque" from the Crown, which entitled them to prey on any enemy ship – and they proved to be good at it. A historic plaque to the "Liverpool Privateersmen" records the exploits in that war, and the War of 1812, of, for example, "Joseph Barss, Jr., of the schooner 'Liverpool Packet' who, in nine months of the War of 1812, captured more than 100 American vessels on the coast of New England." And Enos Collins, the best-known of the Liverpool merchant-privateers, died the wealthiest man in British North America, with nine million dollars to his name. I doubt that Rod or Ed knew much of this when they chose this part of the world for their operation, but you might say that there's a history of fortunes being made at sea around here.

As part of our daily Liverpool routine we'd drive the couple of hundred yards across the bridge to the Stemco shipyard. Ed would check closely on what the workmen were doing, and where needed he'd give them instructions. I was impressed by his technical knowledge. I had been around boats all my life, but I didn't know nearly as much about mechanical works as he did.

I really liked Ed. He was a charming guy, and I got to like him better than any of the other smugglers. Smooth and well-spoken, he had a courtly manner more suggestive of a lawyer than of a sea captain. He was good at anything he touched as far as boats were concerned. Elaine liked him, too, and he was the only person of the bunch about whom we felt badly, knowing he would go to jail. (Although I must admit that over time I also developed a certain fondness for Rod.) Elaine once said that to Chris Paley, and Chris promptly launched into an earnest speech.

"Dope smugglers always seem that way. They never get their hands dirty, and most of them are model prisoners. But don't ever forget what they're doing, and what their drugs do to people. These are bad guys." He was obviously worried that we were getting too emotionally involved with the bad guys.

Ed didn't look like a bad guy. He told me his hair was dyed and that he had shaved off a moustache. I presumed he wanted to change his appearance while doing the job for Rod and then return to his normal looks when he went back home. But later I found out that he was a fugitive from the United States, where he was wanted for a previous hash smuggling escapade.

As we became friendlier, Ed told me he'd handled salvage from some big ships, mostly in South America, recovering ingots as well as propellers and shafts from some major wrecks. He also told me that once he had bought and refitted a surplus U.S. destroyer and then sold it in South America. I have no way of knowing whether that was true, but he certainly was an expert on anything around the water.

Ed not only supervised the refit. At the same time, he started to make other preparations for the drug drop. For a start he asked me to buy a Zodiac inflatable boat with a Suzuki outboard motor. It had to be a 33-horsepower high-turbo engine, and he had detailed specs for the Zodiac as well, since this was the most reliable boat and motor combination for our purpose.

"They're very useful craft as tenders between our boats," he told me. "Sometimes the weather is bad out in the ocean and you can't tie your boat up along the freighter. That's when you need the Zodiac." He sounded like a man who knew what he was talking about, another indication that drug smuggling had its own well-established routine.

I found the right type of motor at a marina in Mahone Bay and paid $3,300 for it. The inflatable Zodiac cost around six thousand dollars. It was a tidy sum, but compared to the *Lady Sharell*'s original price and her refit, it was pretty small potatoes. I was learning that drug smuggling was a business that required a sizable investment.

We brought the Zodiac to my house, and Ed started to work in our garage getting it inflated and putting it together. The process took the better part of a week, and he worked away at it all day every day. Once in a while he'd come upstairs and have coffee with Elaine and me, and she made him supper a couple of times. He was friendly and relaxed, and he didn't suspect a thing. Once, when our stereo broke down, he helped Elaine fix it.

Both the girls asked about Ed since he was around for nearly a week and they heard us mentioning him for much longer than that.

"He's a guy from the States who's going to take the *Lady Sharell* to Sable Island to look for wrecks," I told them. "He's fixing up the Zodiac to be a lifeboat." That seemed to satisfy the girls, and it was a good cover story to use on other occasions, including at the shipyard. Sable Island, some two hundred miles east off the coast of Nova Scotia, is known for its wild ponies but is even better known as a graveyard of ships. Scores of wrecks lie on the bottom there under the fine sands, and a lot of people go looking for them. So the story was entirely plausible.

•   •   •

Ed and I were now spending a lot of time together, with the daily trips to the boatyard, lunches and dinners, and the assembly of the Zodiac at our house. As time went on, he opened up to me a great deal more than Rod ever did. I had a feeling that Rod, who was friendly enough, deliberately never told me one thing more than what I needed to know. I guess he must have thought I was a bit slow, because our talks over meals usually consisted of him repeating over and over what we were doing and what our plans were. I guess I fuelled that by playing dumb and letting him do the talking. I always tried to make him feel that he was teaching me things – which, of course, he was.

There was one big exception to this. Sometime during April, Rod arrived while Ed was busy with other things, and we went to dinner alone. I could sense right away that something was bothering Rod. When we sat down to eat he told me that his brother had just died tragically.

"My brother died a hero," he said, nearly choking on the words. "He was with the Miami fire department, and he died rescuing a child from a car that fell into a canal."

Miami is full of canals, he explained, and the Miami fire department has a special squad of divers to deal with cars that fall in.

"This time my brother's squad arrived on the scene and there was a child in the car. He decided not to wait for the divers and leaped into the water. He never came up again." Rod was clearly shaken by his brother's death. As he told me the story, I was moved, too, and told him I was deeply sorry. But I also wondered how Rod's parents would feel after the arrests, when they found out their other son was a drug smuggler. I felt very sorry for them, too. But I felt I had to get on with the job I had set for myself. If I didn't, a lot of other people's children would end up using drugs. And they, too, deserved pity.

Except for that one instance, Rod was pretty well all business. From the start, my relationship with Ed was much more pleasant. I learned a lot about his life. He told me that he liked the outdoors a great deal, and for relaxation enjoyed spending time in Colorado. He had a ski lodge there, high in the mountains, he said, and had a friend who owned a camp on an even higher peak. To get away from it all, Ed said he liked to take his wife out there and they would ride horses to his friend's camp, where they would go elk hunting.

"There's nothing like the mountains to get away from the rat race," he told me. "It's really quiet and peaceful in Colorado, and I find it regenerates me whenever I get run down."

The rat race – the drug business – paid Ed so well that he had his own airplane to fly to his Colorado getaways. It was an older model – I presumed a bit of a collector's item – and he said he worked on the engines himself and did a lot of the other maintenance. I had no trouble believing that, or that he did all the mechanical work on his Cadillac as well.

He once admitted to me that his wife and son were also in the drug business. His wife acted as a courier, and he was planning to fly her up to Nova Scotia once we picked up the load, when he planned to take some of the stuff to Montreal and other cities.

One of the *Lady Sharell*'s crewmen later told me that Ed used to be a pretty straight guy. He ended up in the drug business when his son and some of his friends planned a smuggling venture, and Ed heard about it and decided to give them a hand with the logistics. I guess he liked it, or maybe he just liked making the money. He certainly enjoyed planning an operation like this one.

Ed also revealed snatches of information about Rod's operation. He indicated that one of the people financing this venture was a large meat and produce dealer in Miami, who owned a fleet of trailer trucks. Naturally I passed all the details on to the RCMP, and I think they had the DEA follow it up. But no indictments were ever issued at that end of the operation.

•   •   •

I soon got my first demonstration of Ed's professionalism and thoroughness. When he finished the assembly of the Zodiac, we put the inflatable and its motor in my half-ton and took it to a boat-launching site right across from Lockeport harbour. Then Ed charted the harbour.

As you'd expect, there are perfectly good marine charts available, but Ed decided not to trust them and to make his own. He was going to have to steer the *Lady Sharell* into Lockeport when the shipment arrived, and he wanted to make sure that there were no hitches with a secret cargo worth millions on board. If I'd been doing the job, I'd have checked out the charts and used them to get the boat to the dock. But not Ed.

It was still pretty nippy the day we did the survey – it was mid-March – and a high wind was blowing. But Ed wouldn't be dissuaded. We were both chilled clear to the bone despite our warm sweaters and some heavy floater jackets. It seemed to take hours to crisscross the entire harbour area. Ed made a note of every rock, buoy, and shoal and ended up with a detailed chart of the entire area. I couldn't believe the thoroughness. And there was more to come.

About a week later, Ed announced that we had some more surveying to do. He picked me up at the house and we drove to the Halifax airport, where he had chartered a twin-engined plane. This time our trip took us way out to sea over Sable Island to pick a rendezvous point for the *Lady Sharell* and the mother ship.

For some time now we'd been discussing the best place for the boats to meet. Chris Paley and Phil Pitts, my Mountie controllers, had instructed me to try for a meeting place as close to Canadian shores as possible. I was doing my best to influence the smugglers' choice in line with those instructions.

Rod had a list of three possible places. One was Flemish Cap, which is about a thousand miles from Nova Scotia. The other was on the southern Grand Banks, about seven hundred and fifty miles from Nova Scotia, and the third was at Sable Island, some two hundred miles offshore.

The Mounties wanted the Sable Island rendezvous because it would make arrests easier. Aside from the distance their vessels would have to travel, there would undoubtedly be arguments in court about international waters.

"Sable Island is our best choice," I'd say during my meetings with Rod and Ed. "The other two places are so far out that they'll attract attention. There's more of a chance for the *Lady Sharell* to get searched and caught."

I played on Rod's desire to make this a "routine" operation and to avoid attracting attention. I don't know whether Rod preferred the far-away locations, but I gathered that the people who ran the mother ship did. Ed clinched the argument in my favour when he said the *Lady Sharell* was too small to go so far out.

Now Ed and I were going to fly over Sable Island so that he could assure himself that the meeting was feasible there and to pick an exact spot.

Sable Island is a pretty desolate place and a graveyard of ships since time immemorial. But it's definitely Canadian territory, which the Mounties wanted. When Ed picked a spot for the transfer some five miles off the island, I knew they'd be pleased.

·   ·   ·

Shortly before Ed arrived, my search for a stash site finally paid off. Driving along the Jordan Bay Road, near a place called Jordan Ferry, I noticed a For Sale sign on a small farm that was about fifteen or twenty acres and right on Jordan Bay. The house was a few hundred yards from the road and hardly visible from the highway because of trees. While there were neighbours around, the house and the rest of the property were pretty secluded. It was also handy, since it was only about twelve miles from Lockeport. I thought it would serve Rod's purpose.

When I told Rod about it, he took one more stab at trying to talk me into putting it in my name. But I said no. He went off to see some local lawyers and bought the place without my involvement. I don't know whose name was used in the deal, but it wasn't mine.

Rod liked the place from the start. It was neatly hidden away, and the house had a large attic that would hold half the shipment when it came in. So he paid sixty to seventy thousand dollars for the little estate, which was a very good price. When the transfer was completed, Ed left his quarters at the Privateer Inn in Liverpool and moved into the house. Compulsive handyman that he was, he immediately started to fix up the place. He, too, was pleased with it, and began to talk enthusiastically about building an airplane hangar at the end of the bay so they could fly drug shipments in by seaplane. It was certainly feasible, and pretty imaginative. While it wasn't usual for seaplanes to land at Jordan Bay, wealthy Americans had bought places elsewhere in the province over the years and sometimes arrived in private planes. The locals just chalked it up to the ways of city slickers who had too much money for their own good.

•   •   •

After Ed's arrival my daily routine had become even more crowded until I sometimes felt like a whirling dervish. I'd touch base with Ed daily, and we'd go over to the shipyard. There he'd show me what the workers had done the previous day, and then we'd head off to take care of some other piece of business, sometimes going to Yarmouth to pick up equipment that Rod had sent from the States.

Then I'd peel off to phone Chris or Phil and secretly report whatever was happening. They might want to meet or perhaps set up another call from Levi later in the day. Then I'd put in a token appearance at the scrapyard where Jim and Elaine were bravely holding the fort. I'd usually manage a quick bite at home, either a late lunch or early supper.

It was hectic, and it was dangerous. While I like to be active, I was feeling the pressure. To make matters worse, Rod was now showing up more and more frequently to check up on last-minute details. I could see that he was satisfied with our progress and that having Ed there to look after the refit was giving him peace of mind.

One of the key pieces of equipment Ed and Rod bought was a sophisticated radio set-up. They bought the latest-model marine radio sets and put one into the stash site at Jordan Ferry and one at our house. There was also one in Miami. The sets were capable of transmitting and receiving on all the standard marine frequencies, which meant that we could talk and listen to both the *Lady Sharell* and the mother ship. To demonstrate the radio's power, Rod called me from Miami on the set at the stash house. We had an animated but innocuous exchange, babbling on about some boat parts in order not to attract the attention of any unknown listeners. I acted greatly impressed with both Ed and Rod when he returned.

Of course, unknown to them, Chris and three RCMP officers from the technical section had carefully examined the radio set in our basement family room to make sure that they could listen in on all the frequencies covered by the smugglers' set-up. On that occasion Elaine was serving the four Mounties lunch, when she spotted a friend's car driving by. It was an anxious moment ("These four strange men? Oh, just some friends," she imagined herself saying). Fortunately, Elaine's car was out of sight, and the woman kept on going.

Whenever Ed and Rod and I met now we spent the time working out details. Rod kept saying the shipment was coming soon.

•　　　•　　　•

Rod was still wedded to the idea that we should have a Canadian crew for the *Lady Sharell* to make everything look as normal as possible. To dissuade him from the local crew idea, and the risk of entrapment that went with it, I argued that the local fishermen had loose lips and that word was bound to get out. At first he wasn't convinced. He believed that he had a good business proposition and that for enough money even a local crew would keep quiet. He may have been right. With the long history of smuggling on the Nova Scotia coast behind them, people certainly knew how to keep silent if they had to. But I wasn't about to admit that. I also told him that it would be hard to get a skilled crew, one that he could rely on. That also wasn't true. Any crew that could go fishing in the Atlantic in the middle of winter, stay out for sixteen or eighteen days, and haul in tons of fish could certainly pick up a few sacks of hash off Sable Island in the middle of the night.

Unexpectedly, Ed came to my rescue. It turned out that he had a group of crewmen he'd worked with before, and he started pressing Rod to let him recruit them.

"They're people I know. I've worked with them before. Why take a chance on strangers?" he said. With two against one, Rod caved in and told Ed to hire the crew he wanted for the *Lady Sharell*.

CHAPTER SEVEN

Looking Ahead

THERE ARE TIMES WHEN I WISH THAT I'D HAD A LITTLE MORE foresight. But back then, as I got more and more involved in this dangerous adventure, I was so caught up in the game – and that's how it seemed – that I never once stopped to work out exactly what would happen to me and my family once the drug ring was arrested, or "taken down," as the Mounties used to say. Day by day, especially since Ed arrived in February 1985, the drug smugglers' investment in this deal was increasing, not only in money but also in time and equipment. The increased activity signalled that D-Day was getting close.

I see now that I should have devoted some time to working out what was going to happen after the Mounties sprung the trap on the mob. But I didn't. I was more interested in obliging the Mounties and in being a good citizen and team player. I admired and respected the two officers I reported to, Chris Paley and Phil Pitts, and later Sergeant Brent Crowhurst, who, as the strike co-ordinator, was next in the chain of command. We had such a close relationship that I trusted them implicitly – and I still do. I guess that's why I never got down in writing exactly what my role was and what was going to happen when the project ended. I was sure that I would be taken care of financially and in other respects.

On more than one occasion I was assured by Chris and Phil, and through them by some of the higher-ups, that I would be "duly compensated" and that we would be taken care of and set up in a new life. It never occurred to me to doubt those assurances. I believed then, as I do now, that they were made in good faith by the men on the spot, who knew what I was going through. But I should have heeded the old saying "Clear treaties make good neighbours."

Looking back on it, I guess the mess-up with the fishing licence should have been a clear warning. In that instance, the Mounties who ran me saw no problem with getting either the licence or the money for it. But once the request got to Halifax and Ottawa, it became another story. It took a near miracle and a great deal of perseverance on my part – not to mention twenty-five thousand bucks of my own money – to pull off the licence deal. Otherwise the whole operation would have died right then and there. From that incident I should have learned that the government bureaucracy doesn't always respond to its servants in the field.

What would the smuggling syndicate do to me once they realized that I had been an undercover agent from the start? Would they seek revenge and put out a contract on my head? What about Rod and Ed personally? Would they go after me once they were out of jail? The RCMP obviously worried about these possibilities, but they had no instant answers. The problem was, our case didn't fit an established pattern. Usually people who go undercover are criminals themselves. They get caught, and they make a deal with the police. Or they're people who want revenge – jilted lovers and such. That wasn't the case with me. I simply didn't like the idea of drugs or anything about them. As far as I was concerned, the rats who brought them into our country should be brought to justice, and I was glad to help the Mounties crack the case.

DEA agent Billy Yout says that he hasn't come across a case like mine either before or since.

"Leonard was an unusual person for us to deal with," he said recently. "In our business, if people co-operate with us, they either want money, they have some other motive, or they are drug traffickers themselves who are trying to stay out of prison. But with Leonard it was different. We had a guy who was unique."

The RCMP also realized that I was different from their usual undercover man, and while the case was under way they treated me extremely well. But I simply assumed that I wasn't unique, that they must be used to protecting honest citizens like me who had worked for them. I was wrong – and I sure should have been more concerned about what was to happen to us after the bust.

I suppose the Mounties could have pretended to arrest me with the smugglers and then released me for lack of evidence. But that wouldn't have accomplished much for me, aside from ruining my reputation in the community. No, I didn't see any way of concluding the operation without my undercover work becoming known to the smugglers. I assumed that I'd have to testify in court at some stage, and I didn't think that Rod, Ed, and the people who were backing them would take too kindly to me, especially if they ended up serving long jail terms.

It looked more and more like we'd have to be given new identities and be relocated. The Mounties first considered taking me away for a few months and leaving the family behind, but Elaine didn't take too kindly to that notion. So they started to think about moving the whole family and changing our identity. Although nothing was laid down and nothing was on paper, there were repeated assurances that I would be "duly compensated," and we assumed that they were planning our new lives.

I wasn't worrying about it. I trusted the Mounties completely, and I was confident that I could succeed wherever I ended up, especially with Elaine at my side. I didn't think the girls would have any difficulty, either. In fact, Sharon seemed rather keen to move. I hinted to her we might just do that, and it was one of the things keeping her at bay in her incessant questioning of Elaine about what was going on.

I knew that the RCMP were giving some thought to our future because early in January 1985 – shortly after our successful family vacation in Daytona Beach – Chris had come to the house and had a long talk with Elaine to make sure she understood what was going on and some of the possible consequences.

By then the Mounties knew me well enough to be aware that I never did anything without telling Elaine, day to day, what was going on. The Mounties also knew that she was very much in the picture because she functioned as the telephone clearing centre for the entire nineteen months. She talked not only to the RCMP but also to the smugglers, which called for a lot of savvy and skill. As far as I was concerned, she was as much an undercover agent as I was.

One of the things Chris had come to find out was how well Elaine and the others in the family would cope during the difficult months ahead. Elaine's a very strong person, and as they were going through some options of what we might do after the bust, she startled Chris when she said suddenly: "As long as we're considering everything, what happens if Leonard gets killed?"

"Chris nearly died when I said that," Elaine recalled later. "He'd never thought of it, and he really got upset."

I wasn't surprised at Chris's reaction. He's a very sensitive man and was always very concerned about the welfare and safety of me and the family. Elaine's question must have hit him like a bombshell. But he also must have realized that Elaine had pinpointed a realistic possibility.

Before the scheduled "takedown," or arrest, of the ring members, no one could really predict how the end would come. But there was a possibility of violence. Rod and Ed may have been pleasant in their everyday dealings, but they were professionals at their big-league game. It was also emerging that the shipment that was coming – it was supposed to be the first of many – would be of considerable size. There had to be big money backing Rod, and money in the drug trade meant muscle power and potential violence.

Chris didn't have an instant answer to Elaine's question, but I'm sure he took the message back to headquarters. Neither Elaine nor I ever did find out what provisions were made in the event of my death. I'd never given it a thought, and I was sure that since I was working for the Mounties Elaine and the kids would be taken care of.

As later events showed, I shouldn't have been so quick to assume things. It wouldn't have hurt to have had a written contract with the RCMP covering some of these eventualities. Sure, I was working for them undercover, but Elaine might have had a tough time proving that if anything had happened to me. Since Ed's arrival I was working on the drug project full time, yet I had no status as an employee with the RCMP. If I'd been killed, it could have had terrible financial consequences for my family. As usual, Elaine had identified a major problem before I did. But we never did do anything about it. If I were doing such a thing today, I'd have a written contract, vetted by my own lawyer. That's one thing I learned from my experience.

.   .   .

Knowing what I know today, I also wouldn't be so quick to agree to moving out of a community where I was established. It seemed like a good idea when it was first mentioned, and it sounded like a bit of an adventure. But while we never left Canada, it didn't take me long to feel like an exile and miss my home. While there were people in Lockeport who still thought of us as outsiders, we regarded the town and the

South Shore as our home. We'd settled there in the early 1970s after a lot of moving around. Before I met and married Elaine I led an even more nomadic life. Maybe if I tell you about it, it'll help explain the sort of crazy guy who'd get involved in this undercover work.

I was born in the small coastal village of Oyster Pond Jeddore, some forty miles east of Halifax, and I had left home before I turned sixteen. With forty dollars in my pocket I headed straight for British Columbia. I was always curious about the West Coast, and I guess like a lot of young men I wanted to get as far from home as possible to prove to myself that I could survive anywhere. I was big for my age and had no trouble getting a job at a huge lumber camp that employed a couple of hundred people.

"You're going to the green chain," the foreman told me the first day. I went off in the direction where he was pointing and saw a giant chain with lumber rolling out of it just like a steady stream of water. I joined a team of about fifteen men who kept the logs going. It was tough work, but I was proud to be making my first wages at fifteen.

From early on, as you can see, I had an itch for adventure. I guess it was in my blood. All the men in my family were seagoing men – my grandfather, his father, and my father's brother – and they all used to go salt fishing off the Grand Banks, and then they would load up their ships with salt fish and take them to Barbados or South America. They'd sell the salt fish and take on a load of rum and sell the rum all along the Nova Scotia coast. They used to call it rum running. It wasn't illegal in those days, and the term didn't take on its present tinge of illegality until modern customs regulations and Prohibition. By the time I was born in my grandmother's house in 1949, the rum running had died down.

I stayed in British Columbia for about a year, then headed back to Nova Scotia. I worked around Halifax, running heavy equipment and driving concrete trucks, tractors, bulldozers, and the like, before the lure of the sea prevailed and I became a deckhand on a research vessel belonging to the Bedford Oceanographic Institute in Halifax.

Now back in Halifax, I needed a place to stay, and when I heard that a woman from my home town was running a boarding house in Dartmouth, I headed across the bay and took a room there. The family had a daughter named Elaine and, well, we started going out together. About a year later we were married.

I quit the Halifax job then and we piled into our beat-up stationwagon and headed for Ontario, "going down the road" like other young people from the Maritimes heading out in search of jobs. We stopped in Toronto, where my first job was in a gas station, before I started driving a tow truck. I also went to night school and became a certified welder. In the end Nova Scotia lured us back again, and I started fishing.

Soon I heard that the job of lighthouse keeper on isolated McNabs Island at the mouth of Halifax Harbour was open. I applied, and because of my experience with the sea and with heavy machinery I got the job and became the youngest lighthouse keeper on the coast.

Elaine and I liked the lighthouse life. But a near tragedy made us leave it. Our oldest daughter, Sharon, was born while we tended the lighthouse. During our first winter there, baby Sharon became very ill with pneumonia and we knew we had to get her to hospital. But a big storm was brewing outside and we had an awful job getting her to the mainland. When we finally made the crossing Sharon had to spend a couple of weeks in hospital. After that Elaine and I decided that we couldn't continue the lighthouse life with an infant.

So we moved back to Halifax, and I started driving heavy equipment again, mostly concrete trucks. Then we lived in Jeddore at Elaine's father's house, but I found it hard to live by the sea and not get involved with it somehow. Before long a new opportunity came up. Elaine's uncle, Art Dooks, was the lighthouse keeper at Gull Rock off Lockeport harbour. I got a job relieving him, and pretty soon I found myself working there for a month at a time – a month on and a month off. It wasn't as big an operation as the McNabs Island lighthouse, and because you can see Gull Rock clearly from shore, we felt safer than at McNabs Island.

Naturally, working at the lighthouse, I was in close touch with fishermen, and one of them told me about the new offshore lobster fishing industry. As you'll have gathered, I like the opportunity to do something new, to get in at the start of what might turn out to be a new industry. So I talked it over with Elaine, and we packed up our belongings and moved to Lockeport.

But I didn't give up the lighthouse work entirely. I continued to work as the relief lighthouse keeper until I got involved with fishing full time. I always kept my eyes open for other opportunities, however; fishing was taxing and dangerous work. In Lockeport a fishermen's monument – a wheelhouse nestled inside a horseshoe-shaped wall made of rocks – not only marks the disastrous loss of three trawlers in 1961 that orphaned more than fifty children but also honours all the local men lost at sea over the years. Each Canada Day a memorial service is held at the site. Many of the town's older houses have built-in markers of the toll the sea has claimed over the years. They each have a balcony-like walkway on their roofs, popularly known as the 'widow's walk.' From there fishermen's wives would keep watch for the returning fleet. All too often some of the boats would not come back.

That's why I always kept my eyes open for business opportunities that didn't involve going to sea. I eventually found one in Shelburne Scrap and Metal, an enterprise I'd built into a profitable business with the help of Elaine and Jim. Our fine new seaside house was testimony to our success.

When the drug caper started, I quickly became so obsessed with making it all work out that I never stopped to think of all the consequences. I had a lot to lose, but I never thought much beyond the RCMP assurances that I would be "duly compensated." At first it meant only compensation for the terrible disruption in our lives. But as the possibility opened up of moving away altogether and giving up our business and our home, "duly compensated" took on a whole new meaning.

CHAPTER EIGHT

Into High Gear

HALIFAX, THE "WARDEN OF THE NORTH," IS A GRAND OLD CITY with an impressive history as a naval base and many impressive old buildings to match. The Holiday Inn on Robie Street was not one of them and didn't seem like a proper setting for a dramatic meeting of major international drug smugglers. It's an average sort of hotel. By Holiday Inn standards it's handsome, but it doesn't have the elegance of some of the hostelries along the city's renovated waterfront, known as the Historic Properties, including the warehouse of Enos Collins, the old Liverpool privateer. Robie Street is inland, and the Holiday Inn, like its namesakes, is functional and clean and pretty anonymous. I'm sure that's why Rod picked it as our regular Halifax meeting place.

Rod and I met there whenever he travelled from Montreal back to Miami and didn't want to drive all the way to Yarmouth or Shelburne to see me. Our meetings were always cordial and brief, and usually over dinner. I would quickly cover with him all the developments in the refit or the stash places. (Now, incidentally, the scrapyard was involved. Rod wanted me to stow half of the first shipment there.) After my report he seemed satisfied and always gave me a verbal pat on the back like, "It won't be long now. Just keep up the good work."

When there was no business on the agenda he would go on about his sailboats in Miami. Another recurring theme of our table talk was food and health.

The *Lady Sharell*'s refit was rolling right along under Ed's supervision. Early in April Ed made a brief trip home to Florida. When he returned he told me, "I've got a crew for the *Sharell*, and they'll be coming up here soon."

I was greatly relieved. Now it was certain that the drug pick-up run would be an all-American operation.

At our next meeting Chris and Phil greeted the news with enthusiasm and started to gear up for action. The countdown had begun.

One day near the end of April Ed announced the crew's arrival. "They'll come to Halifax at the end of the month, and we'll go up to meet them. Rod'll be there, too." He told me we'd all stay the night at the Robie Street Holiday Inn and then drive the crewmen down to the stash house at Jordan Ferry.

When I reported this plan to Chris and Phil, they decided to try to wire the hotel rooms again and went off to alert their technical section to bug the meeting. At this point neither the RCMP nor the American DEA had a fix on who Ed was. They thought the name he was using was phoney, but they weren't able to pin down their suspicions. They were hoping that the meeting with the crewmen would provide some clues.

Rod and Ed went to the airport to pick up the new men,

and we all met at the hotel's bar before having dinner in the restaurant. The crewmen were not an impressive bunch. Like Ed and Rod, all were from the Florida keys and had been around boats. There was Maurice (Scotty) Germaine, a forty-five-year-old who seemed to know Ed the best. He was the one who told me that Ed first got into the drug business through his son. The other two were Robert Barnett, a fifty-eight-year-old car salesman and the most subdued of the lot, and David Tuthill, an exuberant thirty-five-year-old who seemed to be involved in boats or fishing in the Florida keys. They all knew Ed from previous ventures in Florida, and Ed was happy to see them because he could now relax. He had his team and wouldn't have to depend on strangers.

We had adjoining rooms, and conversation continued until everyone went to sleep. I don't know how much hard information the RCMP got out of their bug, but I suppose every little bit helped. The next day we headed to the Jordan Ferry stash place. It was clear that the trio expected to stay only a few days, since none of them had more than one suitcase. They settled into the stash site, and I could see security problems with them right away.

For one thing, they looked like people from Florida. They just didn't blend into the scenery at Jordan Ferry. They dressed like Florida people in colourful clothes and, compared to the locals, they were loud.

Ed tried to control them, keeping them busy fixing up the stash site, but it was difficult. They liked being outdoors, and I could see that they missed the warm Florida sun. Every chance they got they stripped to the waist, and whenever the sun was out for a while they'd rush out to sunbathe. I gathered that at home they liked the bar life, and Shelburne County is just not a busy place for that sort of thing. They'd sneak away to one of the two taverns at Shelburne, but by and large it was difficult to keep them amused.

One day when I drove to the stash site I saw two of them jogging by the side of the highway. They had their shirts off and sweatbands around their heads. As you'd imagine, they didn't look much like the local farm folk. I freaked out and spoke to Ed about it. He told them to cut it out, and they did.

As I've mentioned, Shelburne County is used to tourists, of course. But April and May is not the tourist season, and I didn't want to alert the locals that something unusual was going on. It might have blown the whistle on the whole operation. By now I had a lot of time and emotional energy tied up in this thing, and I wanted it all to unfold according to plan – the Mounties' plan, that is.

The *Lady Sharell*'s refit was now nearly complete. One of the final modifications was to cut a hole in her stern. It was done on Ed's instructions and design and was intended to make it easier to load her at sea. Of course, no one at the shipyard was told its true purpose. As far as they were concerned, the *Lady Sharell* was going to salvage wrecks at Sable Island.

Meanwhile I continued to make my daily rounds, meeting Ed at the shipyard and then heading off to the stash site to talk with him and the crewmen. They were getting a bit restless, and I gathered from Ed that the schedule was running behind. I even heard him talk to Rod on the phone, discussing whether the crewmen should go back to Florida and come up when things were ready.

I asked Rod about that the next time we spoke, and he said: "No, keep everyone in place."

•   •   •

About a week after the crewmen arrived, Rod again asked me to meet him in Halifax. He had a room at our old standby, the Robie Street Holiday Inn.

"It's going to happen very soon," he said as soon as I walked in. "Within a few days we're going to have a final run-through here in Halifax. I'll let you know exactly when and where."

He was still playing the "need to know" game that, I guess, had made him a major drug player at the age of thirty, but I could see that the hawk-like face was tenser than usual when he added: "Tell Ed to have the *Lady Sharell* ready to sail on Monday, May 13. That's a week today."

I stayed cool, but I could hardly contain my excitement.

But the show-and-tell wasn't over yet. Rod had money for me. I was expecting him to give me fifty thousand dollars to pay the final refit bill at the Liverpool shipyard. This he did. But he also handed me a separate envelope, which turned out to contain fifteen Canadian thousand-dollar bills. And he said: "Give these to Ed. They're for the captain of the ship we're expecting. It's his emergency fund in case the ship needs fuel or supplies."

I looked at the money and stuck it in my pocket without counting it. I could hardly wait to get back home and report these startling new developments to Chris and Phil. But first Rod and I went to get something to eat, so it was late by the time I got home and called Chris and Phil. They took down all the information, particularly the sailing date. I expected them to set up a meeting so that they could write down the serial numbers of the bills. They'd always logged the serial numbers of any bills Rod gave me, and I was sure that they'd jump at the chance this time. I was wrong. Neither seemed very keen to meet me, as if they couldn't see any reason for a meeting just to write down serial numbers. I'm sure they also had a big load of arrangements to make and reports to file to their bosses, now that the sailing date had been set. I knew that the RCMP and the DEA had various plans in place, and a great many people were involved. Since Chris and Phil were the main source of information for the whole huge team, they must have been very much in demand.

I had a feeling that it was very important to take down the numbers of these particular bills. After all, they were to be given to the captain of the mother ship – the freighter bringing the drugs – and they could prove to be a key piece of evidence. So I called Chris back and insisted that it was important to take down the numbers. Chris agreed, and the two of them came to the old ammo dump meeting place the next morning, the seventh of May, in an unmarked car. Chris, sitting in the back seat of the car, wrote down the numbers and handed them to Phil, who looked them over and gave them back to me. I don't know whether I had convinced them or whether they thought that I would just keep on pestering them if they didn't agree.

Chris and Phil asked me to keep my ear to the ground for the date and place of Rod's final run-through. I agreed, but I didn't have much of a chance to give them a great deal of notice. Rod called me just before noon on Saturday, May 11, to tell me that the meeting was set for the next day, just a day before the *Lady Sharell* was to sail. Unfortunately Rod didn't say where in Halifax the meeting would take place, and even said it might be in Dartmouth. I was told that it would be at the usual Holiday Inn only a few hours before Ed and I drove off for Halifax, and this didn't give the RCMP enough time to get their bugging gear in place.

Sunday traffic on Provincial Highway 103 was light as Ed and I drove to Halifax. We'd decided to take only one vehicle, so Ed came by the house and picked me up in the blue pickup truck that the gang had bought to tool around Nova Scotia. It took us only two and a half hours to reach Robie Street and the Holiday Inn. We checked into our reserved room. Soon Rod arrived, with a new man in tow carrying a chart case.

The new man's name was Tony, and he seemed to know Ed well. Rod and Ed called him Mr T. He was just a young fellow, no more than twenty-two or twenty-three, and he was a vain smartaleck, a Mr Know-it-all, and I came to dislike him a lot. As he walked in with Rod, who had picked him up at the airport, he had a knapsack on his back and wore a sports-jacket and blue jeans. He also had a half-beard like they have on "Miami Vice" and even imitated the manner and speech of the people on the show. I was later told that this was his first time on a job like this.

Tony, it turned out, was of Italian descent, and he bragged that his family was pretty powerful down in Miami. He claimed that his grandfather owned one of the best restaurants in

Miami. DEA agents later took these claims with a grain of salt, but Rod sure gave the impression that Mr T was somehow connected with people who had a big stake in the shipment.

I sensed right away that Tony didn't trust me. He asked all sorts of questions, trying to trip me up. A couple of times Rod and Ed had to step in and say, "Leave Leonard alone. He's all right."

Eventually I learned to handle Tony by flattering him. I got in the habit of asking him for help or advice on something as often as I could. This pleased him, and he eased off some of the pressure. But our relationship was never an easy one.

Whether or not Tony was part of a mob family, he clearly had a message for Rod and Ed. Eyeing me suspiciously, he beckoned Ed and Rod to the opposite end of the room and huddled with them over the chart he had brought. He was obviously telling them about the mother ship that was bringing the cargo of hashish. If he did mention her name, I didn't catch it. All I heard was "Honduras flag." Tony also seemed to be telling Rod about the mother ship's captain. Again, with them huddled together and talking very low, I didn't make out the substance of the conversation.

I was quite annoyed about them excluding me as if I were some kind of spy, but I didn't want to challenge Tony or appear too nosey. It might have needlessly raised their suspicions – something I'd avoided doing all these months.

As Tony prattled on, he became quite animated, and I could see that he was more excited than he'd seemed at first. It may just have been that he dropped his "Miami Vice" cool mask and became just like any twenty-two-year-old out on his first adventure.

As for me, I kept outwardly calm, but I must admit that I was excited, and a bit apprehensive. After all these months of preparation, the climax was near. I felt a tremendous sense of relief that it was finally happening. But I sure had some butterflies in my stomach. I knew that until the RCMP had everything wrapped up, I would be front and centre, right smack in the middle of whatever was going to happen. I knew, too, that the next few days would be the most dangerous for me and my family. But I also knew that it would be the end of all the pressure I had been under for the past nineteen months. There would be no more undercover meetings with the RCMP and no more fears of being discovered.

•   •   •

The meeting covered the remaining points, and I kept thinking how routine it all was. At least in the old World War II movies they say, "Gentlemen, synchronize your watches." These weren't gentlemen, true, but even the trappings weren't there. It was more like a meeting of vacuum cleaner distributors. All routine stuff.

Then Rod produced some radio codes, a series of call letters and frequencies. Again, I wasn't included in the conversation. I didn't get the codes until Ed gave them to me the next day. It was more of Rod's "need to know" procedure. But Ed passed them on because I'd have to know the codes in order to monitor any exchanges with the mother ship. I had to know when the *Lady Sharell* was headed back, since my job was to meet her at the dock and pick up the crew – and then to get out of the way of the RCMP.

The gang's sophisticated radio link-up, which Ed had put into place months ago, was now going to get a full workout. There was a set at the Jordan Ferry stash site for Rod and Tony to listen to, and I had one in my basement. The mother ship and the *Lady Sharell* had standard marine radios and could talk to either of us. I remembered Rod talking to me from Miami when we first got the radios, and I assumed there was still an active set down in Florida to be used by whoever was monitoring the operation from there.

Rod and Tony were going to be at the stash site, and contact between them and the *Lady Sharell* was to be made at certain times of day. Rod told Ed, who would be manning the *Sharell*'s set, that there wasn't to be a lot of chitchat.

"Keep it to 'Positive' or 'Negative' to let us know whether you've made contact," he instructed Ed. "No idle talk. No small talk. No jokes. When you make contact with the freighter, you'll say 'Discovery, discovery' to let us know. Your code name is Lady D."

My part in the enterprise was pretty straightforward. Once the *Lady Sharell* docked at Lockeport, I was to pick up the three crewmen and drive them to the airport in Yarmouth, where they would catch the next flight for Boston and then to Miami. I would know when the boat was due because I'd either hear it on the radio in my basement or at the stash site, where Rod and Tony would be monitoring at the set times.

Rod also gave Ed the exact co-ordinates of the meeting place off Sable Island. While Ed and I had picked the spot during our survey flight, the skipper of the mother ship had to approve them. And Tony seemed to be the link to him.

According to Rod's estimate, the freighter would arrive at the rendezvous site at daybreak on Wednesday, May 15, giving the *Lady Sharell* two days at sea before the meeting. It all seemed very simple and uncomplicated.

Ed and Rod also decided that the *Lady Sharell* should pick up a load of ice. This was to be put on top of the hashish once it was in the hold. Any passerby would be sure to think that there was a load of fish underneath.

As soon as the meeting ended, just before 9 P.M., Ed jumped into the blue pickup and drove off for the Jordan Ferry stash site. He wanted to get a good night's sleep for the journey ahead. He probably also wanted to carry out a bed-check of his crew to make sure they didn't wander off somewhere before the big day. The rest of us adjourned to the Five Fishermen, one of Halifax's best restaurants, for a late supper. Like Rod, wouldn't you know it, Tony turned out to be a vegetarian.

As the food was served, Rod turned his hawk face to me and said, "I think Tony and I will stay in Halifax tonight, perhaps even tomorrow." He didn't give a reason, but maybe the bright lights of Halifax suited them both better than the prospect of spending the night at the Jordan Ferry stash house.

But I also began to suspect that despite what he said, Rod didn't really expect the boats to meet by Wednesday.

Rod was clearly going over details of the operation in his mind and had discovered a potential problem. If we'd all gone back that night as originally planned, I'd be on hand to arrange for the ice for the *Lady Sharell* as she sailed the next morning. Now, Rod worried whether Ed and the Florida crew would arouse suspicion as they stopped to pick up ice. He had a point. Local people are very protective of their fishing rights, and if they see a strange vessel, or a vessel with a strange crew, pull in, they'll break a leg to call inspectors from the federal Department of Fisheries and Oceans. If the crew turn out to be poachers, they're in trouble. If the inspectors smell drugs, they call the RCMP. A lot of drug boats get caught that way. I knew that the closest place to get ice for the *Lady Sharell* was at Mersey Seafoods in Liverpool harbour, just across from where she was tied up at the dockyard. And a Florida crew would sure have been noticed.

"You've got to get back there and help Ed buy the ice," Rod told me. "We'll get a taxi for you – and you take it back to Jordan Bay. No expense spared." That's what we did, and I set off in a Halifax cab on the two-and-a-half-hour journey.

It was fine with me, because I didn't want to miss seeing the *Lady Sharell* sail. After all, it was the start of the final round of my work for the RCMP, and I felt I owed it to myself to see her head out to sea. In a funny kind of way, I'd come to love her by then, and while I coveted nothing that the smugglers owned, I did have a secret hope that I could some-how end up owning her.

·   ·   ·

The taxi ride seemed to take forever. I've driven from Halifax to Lockeport and other South Shore towns more times than I care to remember and know each nook and cranny in the highway and just about every gas station and restaurant along the way. Sitting in the passenger seat and being driven was a new experience for me, and I guess that's why it seemed to take so long. The fare was a hundred and ten dollars, which the driver, a fine Nova Scotian, accepted without comment.

Ed was still up when I entered the stash house. It was after midnight, and I was tired.

"Rod sent me down to get the ice with you tomorrow," I told him. "I'm going home, and I'll see you first thing in the morning. All you have to do is to slide the *Lady Sharell* across the bay to Mersey Seafoods, and I'll make all the arrangements. Then you can head out to sea."

Ed told me to use the blue pickup to get home. As I drove off, I noticed that the chart was lying across the dashboard in the truck. I got all excited and phoned Chris as soon as I got home. It was now 2 A.M.

"Should I open it up and have a look?" I asked him.

"No, don't touch it!" he said, coming awake fast. "They might notice if you opened it up. Why take a chance on blowing it now?"

I said good-bye and crashed into bed, exhausted.

CHAPTER NINE

Twelve Days to Takedown

My alarm jarred me out of a deep sleep at five in the morning. It was Monday, May 13, the *Lady Sharell*'s sailing day. I quickly showered and shaved and jumped into the blue pickup that Ed had loaned me the night before. In fifteen minutes I was at the Jordan Ferry stash house, where Ed and his three crewmen were all ready to go.

I helped them load their bags into the truck. A couple of them had to ride in the back because we couldn't fit everyone into the half-ton's cab, and it was lucky that they had only one bag each. There wasn't much conversation. None of the crew were morning people. But I could see they were happy that things were moving. They'd been waiting for two weeks in the isolated little farmhouse, expecting to stay only a few days, and they'd been getting awfully bored.

As we drove off, Ed pulled a piece of paper out of his shirt pocket and gave it to me. It contained the radio frequencies and call letters that I'd use to monitor the *Lady Sharell*'s progress. I tucked the paper away and drove directly to the shipyard in Liverpool where the *Lady Sharell* had just completed her second refit. Tied to the wharf all ready to go, newly painted green and white with an oversize Canadian flag gracing her bow, I'll tell you, she was a sight to see. She had really been nicely fixed up, and it was obvious that people at this shipyard knew what they were doing. Of course, Ed had seen to it that they did their best.

While the crew was boarding her, I got back in the truck, drove across the small bridge that spans the harbour just next to the shipyard, and stopped at Mersey Seafoods. I had already called them from home about a load of ice for the *Lady Sharell*, and everything was ready.

I watched from the wharf as, at exactly 7:45 A.M., Ed started her engines and gently eased her out of the refit yard. The weather couldn't have been better. It was the finest kind of morning, with the sun just beginning its daily climb and the water as still as a mirror. The *Lady Sharell* broke the calm as she moved easily across the harbour to the Mersey Seafoods wharf. I caught their line, and she tied up while the crew placed the load of ice in her hold. A blue tarpaulin was thrown over it before the hatches were closed up. Her tanks had been topped up, and Ed had stocked her with groceries, and now she was ready to go. I found myself calling out to wish Ed luck as he headed out. Not another boat was moving in the harbour as she headed for the open sea at exactly 8:20 A.M.

I hopped back in the truck and drove to Mersey Point at land's edge and sat there in the cab of the truck, watching her until she was out of sight.

•   •   •

Everyone knows from television that the Lebanese port of

Tripoli bears the scars of a decade of civil war. The streets are lined with the rubble of bombed-out buildings and wrecked cars. But since Lebanon came into my life, in a way, I've learned a bit about it, and I know that the port is busy despite the war. Tons of cargo are being handled here. Incoming are luxury goods from France and Japan. Outgoing is Lebanon's main export: drugs, especially hashish. Drug boats leave at regular intervals for Western Europe or North America. And the revenue they generate keeps the economy of war-torn Lebanon afloat.

Dozens of nondescript freighters leave Tripoli regularly, headed for secret rendezvous with smaller ships off the coasts of Europe or North America. In fact the port of Tripoli is regarded as a major starting point of the international drug pipeline. And Lebanon itself is seen by police forces around the world as a major supplier to the West especially of hashish, but also of heroin. According to official RCMP statistics, about 70 per cent of the hashish and hash oil imported into Canada in 1985 originated in Lebanon.

On April 16, 1985, almost exactly a month before I watched the *Lady Sharell* disappear from my view into the Atlantic, the coastal freighter *Ernestina* set sail from Tripoli. The *Ernestina* was only about 180 feet long. Her hull was painted red and her superstructure white, and the lettering at her stern showed her home port was San Lorenzo, Honduras. In her hold was 13.361 tons of hash resin, compressed into oval blocks of about two pounds each. The cargo was split into 453 bales with twenty-four or twenty-five blocks in each bale. Thirteen tons was not a lot of cargo for a ship that size, and she was riding high in the water. But for a cargo of hash it was pretty large, even by Lebanese standards.

This was the vessel that Rod had hired in his travels overseas. The details of the arrangements were never made public, and he certainly never told me. But some of the police think the deal was made through Amsterdam and that the *Ernestina* had a previous connection with the Dutch port. She's said to have been used to transport drugs from Syria to Europe.

The cargo of hashish in her hold likely came from the Bekaa Valley, better known to the outside world as the base of radical Shi'a Moslem sects and the probable prison of Western hostages. The area, which used to be poor, is now thriving on drug money and is controlled by the drug clans. No police force in the world ventures there. Syrian military forces officially control the Bekaa and most of Lebanon, but one of the few Western journalists to visit there recently reported that the occupation hasn't put a damper on the drug trade. At checkpoints at every crossroads, the Syrians extract a transportation tax from drug-carrying truck convoys.

Even the bitter Moslem-Christian fighting that goes on there is no obstacle. Much of the hashish is grown by Moslem farmers, who have to cross Christian areas to reach the sea, including the port of Tripoli. Christians and Moslems regularly massacre each other's villages in the Bekaa. Yet they cooperate in the drug trade. The trade's capital is Baalbeck, a Moslem city and also the centre of Shi'a radicalism. Here, the drug clans who control the valley fill huge barns with harvested hashish plants to let them dry. Because of the prosperity that the trade has brought, the sifting and grading has become mechanized, which allows the hash resin to be compressed into the oval slabs of the type that made their way aboard the *Ernestina.*

The day before the *Ernestina* sailed a twenty-two-year-old Syrian, Malik Solayman, walked around the port of Tripoli asking for a ship going to Cyprus. According to the story he later told to a Canadian court, someone directed him to the *Ernestina.* Solayman didn't find her Honduran registration unusual, since a great many ships along the Mediterranean coast are registered in flag-of-convenience countries. Solayman said he met the captain, who introduced himself only as George, and told him that the ship would leave for Cyprus shortly.

"It was to go to Cyprus and take cargo from there back to Tripoli," Solayman recalled. He signed up as a seaman at a pay of five hundred dollars u.s. per month. But Solayman claimed that he intended to leave the ship in Cyprus and look for a summer job on the island. He was an experienced seaman, he said, but he worked on ships only during the summer because he was studying law at Damascus University. He had documents to show that he was in the third year of a four-year course.

Solayman went aboard the *Ernestina* around 5 P.M. on April 15 and met the other members of the crew – a Lebanese and four Syrians. They were Mohammed Chawiche, the senior member of the crew, Moustafa Ammar, the cook, Moustafa Chawiche, the chief engineer, and Malik Dekmak, a young sailor. Because one of the five crew cabins was filled with food and supplies, Solayman was assigned to share a cabin with Mohammed Chawiche. Small freighters, especially Arab ones, are quite informal, and Solayman was pleased to be on this one.

The next morning, however, Captain George gathered the crew around him and announced that there had been a change of plan. "He informed us that he was no longer going to work on the ship, and he told us that there would be a second captain, a new captain coming," Solayman recalled. The crew took the news with a shrug and went about their assigned tasks of cleaning, polishing, and cooking. Around 4 P.M. the ship moved from the dock to ride at anchor in the harbour.

It was well after dark – around 10 P.M. – when a tender with three men pulled up to the *Ernestina*. Three men clambered aboard. One of them introduced himself as a Mr Fouez and asked the crew to assemble. He then announced that one of the men with him, Harry Sunila, was the new captain.

"He said it was the first time that the captain had any dealings with Arabs and that's why the third man, Abdul Karim, would be the captain's mate and would be the captain's liaison with the crew," Solayman recalled. Fouez then added: "I would like you to act nicely to the captain and give him your full co-operation. The captain would like to sail right away."

With that, the mysterious Fouez climbed back down into the tender and headed off in the darkness back to shore.

It only took ten or fifteen minutes to get the *Ernestina* under way. Solayman and his roommate, Chawiche, raised the anchor and were freed to their cabin to sleep as the ship set sail.

The next day, the crew put in a full day's work. From experience – he'd made the trip more than twenty times – Solayman knew that the crossing to Cyprus should take eighteen hours, certainly no more than twenty. By his calculations, the *Ernestina* should have reached Cyprus by about 6 P.M. on April 17. But the *Ernestina* did not arrive in Cyprus at 6 P.M., or at 8 P.M., or even at 10 P.M. By then Solayman realized that the lights of Cyprus were behind them. The ship had passed the island.

According to Solayman's account, the crew argued among themselves about it, and since there had been no announcement from the captain, Solayman sought out Abdul Karim, the Arabic-speaking mate.

"There's been a change of plan. We're going to Morocco," Karim told him. But before the *Ernestina* reached Morocco, Solayman overheard a conversation indicating that the captain had received new instructions again, and that the ship was now heading to a destination in the Atlantic.

Asked many months later what his reaction was, Solayman said, "I felt afraid. I felt scared. I felt everything because I have heard that even large ships don't sail safely through the Atlantic." He said he made his feelings known to Karim.

"The captain has his instructions, and we are obliged to follow them," Karim told him brusquely. "You have to follow instructions, too."

According to Solayman, he wasn't the only one who was uneasy. The other crew members didn't like the idea of the Atlantic any better than he did, and when they pressed Karim for information, he opened his jacket to reveal a pistol tucked into his belt.

In Solayman's words, he warned them, "Don't involve yourself in things that are none of your concern, because you will hear words that will not suit you. All you have to do is to continue to do your job." From then on, Solayman said, he and the crew were very conscious of the gun in Karim's belt. He was never without it. The crew also noticed another addition. A small Soviet-made machine gun was to be seen in the captain's quarters next to a couch where Karim sometimes slept.

Solayman claimed that he neither knew the *Ernestina*'s destination, nor that she was carrying a cargo of dope. He didn't even hear until mid-May what her cargo was and didn't actually see it until the bales of hashish were piled on deck, ready for transfer to the *Lady Sharell*. Up until then, he thought the ship was empty.

A jury in Halifax believed his story and found him not guilty of possession and importation of narcotics into Canada. But veteran DEA agent Billy Yout found the story hard to believe.

"In Miami we get these ships all the time and the first thing out of their mouths is: 'I didn't know anything. I just hired on. We were supposed to be going here, we went there.' " And he had special trouble believing Solayman's story that he didn't know the cargo was hashish. "If you were on the vessel, you'd know it was there, plus the stink – the smell. It's compressed marijuana, and what it does, it gives off the same odour. Fifty days at sea, and he never made it to the cargo hold?"

•   •   •

Immediately after I watched the *Lady Sharell* head out to sea, I called Chris Paley on the phone to read him the radio frequencies and recognition codes that Ed had given me. The stash house radio's code was J7A BBX, and the expected freighter's was KXY. There were other letters and numbers and the two frequencies to be used – 2146 kilohertz and 4125 kilohertz. Then Chris asked me to meet him and Phil Pitts after lunch at the old ammo dump for what would be our last get-together there. They both assured me that everything was on schedule.

"We're going to move your family out tomorrow and you'll join them after the takedown," Chris told me. That was my arrangement with the RCMP. My family would be moved first, and I'd follow once the *Lady Sharell* returned to Lockeport. Rod had said that the boats were to meet out at sea at dawn Wednesday, which meant that the arrests would take place a couple of days later. The RCMP were to look after the safety of Elaine and the girls until the smugglers were in custody. I was to drive Elaine and the girls to the town of Bridgewater, where they would be met by Mounties who would guard them. Once the arrests were made, we'd come back to Lockeport briefly, say good-bye to family and friends, and then leave for a new place with new identities, both to be picked for us by the RCMP – or so we thought.

The day the family was to leave was a Tuesday, and it turned out to be a dramatic day of suspense, joy, and revelation. For the first time Elaine and I would be able to explain to Sharon and Jewell what had been going on. But until the whole thing was over we had to keep it all secret from other people, including family. And that was difficult. For instance, Elaine got a call from her sister, Gayla, asking her to babysit her three children on Tuesday morning. Elaine had a great deal left to do, but she couldn't refuse without arousing Gayla's suspicions. So she agreed and made Gayla promise to pick the kids up before 12:30 in the afternoon, so she could pack before our scheduled departure at 3:30.

"I sent them to the basement to play," she recalled, "and I told them, 'No mess! No mess!' "

To get our own children ready, Elaine dropped Jewell off at school at noon and then looked for Sharon. She spotted her chatting with her best friend, Patricia, and said: "Sharon, after school today we're going to go to New Brunswick for a few days to visit your friend Monica."

Monica was the daughter of our former pastor, and she and Sharon had been best friends.

I decided to pick up the girls myself after school. I took the Cadillac, our family car, instead of the pickup, and Sharon found that unusual.

"What on earth's going on, Dad?" she asked as we drove by the post office to pick up our mail.

"Just wait till we get your mother," I replied. "Now go and pack. But I'll tell you that this is going to be the most important day of your life!"

Sharon had no idea what was coming, but she blurted out: "Are we going to meet Papa Smurf?" While she didn't know what was coming, she somehow sensed that Chris Paley was involved.

So I said, "Yes, you're going to meet him."

Now Sharon and Jewell were really excited, and they hurried their packing. We all got into the car and left our house. We were only about three houses away when Elaine and I couldn't contain our own excitement any longer.

I'll never forget the startled look on their faces when they learned that Chris was an RCMP officer. They were speechless for a moment and then broke into wide smiles. I then explained about my undercover role, and they were stunned. Not only was their father involved in secret and dangerous work with Miami gangsters but their idol, Chris Paley, was a heroic police officer.

I took most of the hour-long drive to Bridgewater to answer the questions they were firing at me. Our meeting with the RCMP was set for a motel called the Wandlyn Inn. As luck would have it, Chris Paley – or Papa Smurf – was at the front door watching for us. The girls were overjoyed.

"I remember I could hardly breathe. My heart was beating so fast," Sharon recalled. "Chris was quiet, more subdued than we were used to seeing him, and he told us, 'We have a room down here.' "

It turned out they couldn't get the conference room, and the room we were in was dark and tiny and there weren't enough chairs for everybody. Chris, Phil Pitts, and Brent Crowhurst sat us around the table, and Chris said to the girls, "I guess your Mom and Dad have told you the story. Is there anything else you'd like to know?

"We're really proud of your father. He's doing a wonderful thing," Chris told the girls, heaping praise till I started to get embarrassed.

He added that Elaine and the girls were now supposed to go with Brent, who would take good care of them, and that soon we would all be reunited. Right now Chris had another task ahead of him. The girls gave him our cat and five kittens to take care of while we were gone, and he promised to do a good job. While he and Phil went to get the kittens out of our car, Brent Crowhurst told the girls and Elaine that they would be going to a hotel called the Oak Island Inn until it was all over.

I was sure that Chris and Phil had left the room on purpose. Just like Rod's "need to know" system, it was part of the RCMP security arrangements that only Brent would know where Elaine and the girls were going. That reduced the risk of any slip-up or of anyone overhearing their whereabouts. I was impressed — and reassured — by that.

The Oak Island Inn is a lovely traditional Nova Scotia tourist hotel. As you'd expect, it overlooks Oak Island, the famous site of a series of deep and unexplained tunnels dating back to the sixteenth or seventeenth century. Over the years scores of treasure hunters have poured millions of dollars into excavating the island in the belief that the biggest pirate treasure trove in North America is buried there. Several people have died probing the mystery of the tunnels, and exploration continues to this day with a ten-million-dollar drilling venture going on as I write.

Everything was ready for them at the Oak Island Inn. They had been pre-registered, and Elaine and the girls had adjoining rooms. A male and a female RCMP officer, Brian and Nicole, were there waiting for them and they all settled down to a calm wait that was expected to last a couple of days until the boat returned to Lockeport, into the arms of the police.

It was a good place for the family to be while the rest of the operation came together, and I knew that they'd be in good hands. Before Chris and I drove off, the Mounties left us alone to say good-bye. There were tears, but I said, "Don't be scared. There's nothing to be scared of."

That seemed to calm their fears. We all joined hands and prayed briefly before parting.

.   .   .

I knew I didn't have to worry about my family, but I was concerned that Rod or Tony would notice that they'd left home and become suspicious. So I rushed back to Lockeport as fast as I could. Since the takedown was supposed to happen in a couple of days, or three at the most, I didn't see any problems if neighbours or Elaine's sisters came by. I could easily explain their absence for a couple of days. The story about going to New Brunswick for a visit was a plausible one.

But as the days rolled on, it became harder and harder to explain to people where my family was, and why. As I'd expected, Elaine's sister Gayla came by on the second or third day and asked, "Where's Elaine? Where are the kids?"

She seemed satisfied when I explained that they were away for a couple of days, but when she came again a day or two later, her tone became more and more accusing. Elaine's other sister, Betty, was constantly on the phone with the same type of questions, pestering me so much that I phoned Elaine at the Oak Island Inn and asked her to call Betty. This made matters even worse. Elaine said she was in Toronto, and when Betty asked to speak to the kids, Elaine said, "They can't come to the phone right now. They're at a fair across the street."

Betty knew that Elaine wouldn't let the girls go alone to a fair in Toronto, and this made her even more suspicious.

I could see that all kinds of things were going through their minds. One day I just dozed off on the bed for an hour about three or four o'clock in the afternoon. When I opened my eyes, Gayla was in the bedroom doorway asking, "Where's Elaine?" Then she rushed over to look under the bed, thinking I had another woman hidden there. It occurred to me that the spy heroes you read about never had to deal with that sort of family stuff.

Not only did I have to keep Elaine's sisters at bay, I also had to make sure that Rod and Tony stayed well clear of the house. To do that I had to keep rushing over to the stash site every chance I got, to keep in contact with Rod and Tony, who were manning the radio. And, of course, the RCMP kept wanting to know what was happening. I had to dash off and meet with Chris and Phil from time to time to keep them informed. I was pretty excited myself, and between that and all the bases I had to cover, I didn't get much sleep.

The Mounties had their problems, too. The RCMP tactical team from Halifax – the commando group with guns formally known as the Emergency Response Team – was now hidden in a warehouse, right on the Government Wharf in Lockeport harbour. They had moved in as soon as the *Lady Sharell* had sailed out of sight, and had settled down to make themselves as comfortable as possible during the long wait.

At the stash site a couple of armed Mounties were hidden in the woods, ready to move on Tony and Rod once the *Lady Sharell* had been seized. All in all, this operation involved more than sixty people on the ground. And of course there were the Armed Forces and Coast Guard, too.

From the moment she left the dock at Liverpool the *Lady Sharell* had been tracked by an Aurora anti-submarine plane flying too high to be detected from the ship. The Canadian destroyer *Iroquois* was also in position to move in, and a Coast Guard cutter was lounging in Lockeport harbour, ready to block the *Sharell's* exit if she decided to make a run for it. And these people on the scene were only the tip of the iceberg. An awful lot of people and resources had been thrown into this operation. It was like a huge parade. But the guest of honour was slow in coming.

·   ·   ·

The operation mounted by the RCMP and the military was so big it was no wonder that some of those responsible were getting edgy. And they were – especially in Ottawa. All these men and equipment were on alert twenty-four hours a day, and the fellows behind the desks in Ottawa were adding up the overtime bills. The tension from above filtered down, and even Chris, Brent, and Phil were becoming edgy as "Negative, Negative" crackled out of the radio each day, each night.

No one wanted the ships to meet more than I did. The Mounties may have been worried about costs, but all I wanted was some sleep. I was up day and night, alert for the contact and making sure that Rod and Tony kept away from my house. But night after night, Ed's voice came crackling over the airwaves from the *Lady Sharell*: "Negative, Negative. Nothing today."

On the third day after the expected rendezvous the *Lady Sharell* approached a ship. Though there was no radio traffic to indicate that it was the ship they had been waiting for, the RCMP decided that this was it. And then when the *Lady Sharell* pulled away, apparently having made a mistake, Ottawa decided to wind down the operation. I was very disappointed, and so were some of the Mounties I had worked with, who argued back and forth with Ottawa until they decided not to wind it down completely but to keep it at a low key. The number of police on alert was reduced, though they promised to warm it all up again if the ships made contact.

Chris and Phil had told me that ships sometimes failed to connect. There were two more occasions when the *Lady Sharell* came close to another boat, sending waves of excitement through the ranks of the Mounties, but each time there was more disappointment, and doubts began to grow that the ships would ever meet. The North Atlantic is a huge place, and a lot can happen to a ship between the time it leaves Lebanon with a drug cargo and reaches Canadian shores.

That certainly turned out to be true for the *Ernestina*. While we were all waiting, biting our nails up to the elbows, she had to make a long detour in international waters to avoid some unfriendly ships and now was low on fuel. They were running her very slow just to save the last scraps of fuel.

The days dragged on, without any contact, and the pressure built up everywhere. On board the *Lady Sharell* it must have been worst of all. If the three crewmen were unruly at the stash site, I imagine Ed had his hands full at sea. Here were these guys from Florida, in Nova Scotia for an operation that was supposed to have taken only a few days start to finish. First they had spent two weeks at a farm that must have seemed in the middle of nowhere, and now they were spending about the same amount of time at sea in mostly bad weather. Ed later admitted that he didn't get much sleep and that his supplies were running so low that he thought he might have to turn back.

Finally, in the evening of Wednesday, May 22 – exactly a week later than expected – Ed got a response to his frantic radio call of "Discovery, Lady D, Discovery, Lady D."

·   ·   ·

I wasn't at my radio set when contact was finally made. I was in transit, rushing from a quick meeting with the Mounties to the stash site at Jordan Ferry. When I got to the little house, the activity was feverish. Tony was on the radio jabbering excitedly to a guy on the mother ship, a big smile on his face, and Rod could hardly hide his excitement.

Scanning their radar, Ed tried once more over his radio: "Discovery, Lady D. Discovery, Lady D."

"Hello, sir. Do you copy?" came the response – received by some very happy Mounties.

"Yeah, Roger on that. How you doin', captain?" Ed replied.

"Very good, sir. How you doing?"

"Boy, sure is beautiful out. Understand though it's supposed to give a blow about midnight. Over."

"Yeah, that's when I should be in your neighbourhood, too, sir."

Ed tried out his codes, consisting of letters and some questions and answers about engine parts and then came back with: "Discovery, discovery. We've been looking for you for a long time."

Though the ships were now in radio contact, it would still be several hours before they could see each other. When that happened, it was dramatic. The white superstructure of the 180-foot *Ernestina* came looming out of the dark and fog, its red hull towering over the much smaller *Lady Sharell*. After a period of circling, the two ships slowly converged. With great care — this was the part where wooden ships had come to grief — they came alongside.

RCMP monitors heard the voice of Harry Grant Sunila, thought to be the *Ernestina*'s skipper, say, "Shall we do it here?"

"Yes," came Ed's reply.

"Ready when you are, sir."

"Okay, just stay there," said Ed.

With the ships really close, Ed climbed up and over the gunwale of the *Ernestina* and made his way to the wheel-house. There he handed the chart with the fifteen Canadian thousand-dollar bills attached to it to the *Ernestina*'s captain, and for about fifteen minutes they made final arrangements for the cargo transfer.

As I know all too well from my fishing days, the Atlantic is just about never still. In the rolling ocean swells and the dark and fog it must have been a tricky job to position the *Ernestina* so the *Lady Sharell* could come in, stern first, on her lee, to get the loading operation set up. But the smugglers were up to the task, and the two ships came together.

The hashish had already been brought up and stacked on the *Ernestina*'s deck. Now, braced against the roll of the ship, the two crews worked furiously to transfer the bales down to the *Lady Sharell*, where the men from Miami worked up a sweat stacking the bales in the fish hold and under the ice. The transfer under cover of night took almost exactly an hour.

The two vessels felt very much alone on the ocean off Sable Island. But they were not.

CHAPTER TEN

Springing the Trap

WHEN THE *LADY SHARELL* HEADED OUT OF LIVERPOOL ON MON-day, May 13, looking like any other fishing trawler going about her business, she was the only boat in motion in the mirror-like harbour. But that didn't mean she was alone. She was probably the most closely monitored vessel in the entire history of the South Shore.

Since 3:30 A.M., RCMP Corporal Phil Pitts and Constable Bill Dickie had been watching the harbour through binoculars from the darkened Royal Canadian Legion Building that once had housed an RCMP detachment. Their observation post just across from the Privateer Inn offered the two Mounties a vantage point that overlooked the whole harbour. They were able to watch the *Lady Sharell* start her engines, ease over to the Mersey Seafoods wharf, take on a load of ice, then leave the harbour.

Five miles away, at a place called Scots Bay, Corporal Bryan Hatt of the RCMP's I, or technical support, section, was manning a Furuno Marine Radar with a computer electronic compass and a Loran c navigator. His task was to start tracking the *Lady Sharell* as soon as she left the harbour so that her position could be passed on to the Canadian Armed Forces.

In the air an Armed Forces Aurora submarine surveillance airplane had been hovering over Liverpool since 3:30 A.M., and, according to its tactical navigator, Captain Wilfred E. Perron, its radar and other monitoring equipment became operational a half-hour later. The Aurora was from 415 Squadron based in Greenwood, in Nova Scotia's Annapolis Valley. The air crews who normally patrol Canada's coast had been instructed to help the RCMP carry out surveillance of the *Lady Sharell* – and anyone she might meet. The orders called for "covert surveillance," which meant the military aircraft were to stay out of sight of the ship. Even from high up in the sky, out of the ship's sight, relays of planes were able to track the *Lady Sharell*, neatly handing over the tracking from plane to plane and navigator to navigator, to produce a computer printout of her every move. They recorded her departure, her voyage to Sable Island, and her rendezvous with the *Ernestina* all the way to her return to Lockeport.

The *Lady Sharell*'s steel hull may have been just the thing for a drug offload, but it also provided an easy target for the Aurora's sensitive radar devices, which I'm told can pick out a tiny submarine periscope on the surface of the ocean.

To establish that the aircraft were tracking the right boat, Corporal Hatt's radar and navigation equipment on the ground at Scots Bay logged the *Lady Sharell*'s initial position.

At 9:14 A.M. the first set of co-ordinates giving her position was delivered to the Department of National Defence, to be passed on to the Aurora and matched up with the plane's own observation.

"Forty-four, zero one, zero zero north, sixty-four, thirty-seven, eighty-five west," the liaison man logged. It was the first of dozens of co-ordinates passed on to the Armed Forces until the ship was so far from land that Aurora aircraft took over the mission entirely.

A relay of thirty-eight flights was used, and more than a hundred radar operators tracked the *Lady Sharell* and later the *Ernestina* – represented by tiny boat symbols on their fourteen-inch radar screens – day after day.

It was nine days before anything noteworthy happened. Warrant Officer Donald J. Cook was manning his Aurora's radar when he noticed that a second, larger ship was approaching his target near Sable Island. He testified that the two vessels "converged" and made a circle around each other. Then they got together for fifteen minutes and broke apart, only to come together again for about an hour.

When the ships finally parted, with the *Lady Sharell* heading back for home, Ed must have been a happy man. The transfer of the cargo had taken place without a hitch, the hashish was safely stowed under the ice, and in his pocket was a receipt for his cargo. Now it was a clear sail back to Lockeport.

·   ·   ·

At the Oak Island Inn things had been fine for my family. The girls had been having the time of their lives being entertained by the four RCMP officers assigned to guard them around the clock. They loved it – especially during the first few days, when they went to a local fair three times in the first week. The armed officer who spent the most time with them was named Brian, and, predictably, the girls took a shine to him. Elaine, or course, had less interest in the fair. She spent a lot of time just resting after the months of strain, but she did take in the occasional shopping trip with her bodyguards, Nicole and Karen.

They were kept informed of my progress through my occasional visits – I did manage one overnight stay with them – and through phone calls from me or Chris. And according to Sharon they could have gone on "forever" just being entertained.

But as a week went by without the boats meeting, the strain of waiting in suspense began to affect them, too, especially Elaine. She knew that Chris and I were uptight, and she became a bit nervous as well. Then, when the boats did meet, the Mounties moved them to the Airport Hotel, just outside Halifax, where the tensions increased.

To take the pressure off, they all set up a betting pool on the day of the takedown. The girls, Elaine, and the Mounties each put in two dollars.

Sharon picked Friday, May 24.

·   ·   ·

Until I die I'll remember Friday, May 24, the day the *Lady Sharell* came back to Lockeport. She'd never looked better than when her white superstructure broke through the early morning mist, and she slid smoothly into the harbour, her green hull making only a few ripples on the calm water. A fisherman making an early start for his lobster traps passed her as she eased alongside the public wharf. It was 5:30 A.M.

I'd been up most of the night, laying plans with the Mounties. Once the boats had made contact, the guys behind the desks in Ottawa had got interested again. The operation was back up to strength, and the tactical team – dressed like commandos and armed to the teeth – had been sitting hidden in the warehouse near the water's edge for more than twenty-four hours. We knew for sure the boat was arriving this morning because I'd been in the Jordan Ferry stash house late in the afternoon when Ed had radioed in the message to Rod and Tony that he'd be arriving around 6 A.M. I knew Ed was a good navigator, and I was looking for him to make his estimated time. But Chris and Brent and the other Mounties calculated that the *Lady Sharell* would arrive at 8:30 or 9:00 A.M. That's why Chris, who was supposed to be at my side once the takedown started, wasn't around when the *Sharell* pulled in at daybreak.

Rod had wanted me on the wharf with him. At the Halifax

meeting he'd assigned me to take my car to the dock and drive the crew members to Yarmouth Airport as soon as the *Lady Sharell* docked. This bothered the Mounties a great deal. They didn't want me not showing up at the wharf — that would have made Rod suspicious. But they sure didn't want me to stay on the wharf, because they were afraid that bullets might be flying around there, and they wanted me out of the line of fire. The Mounties knew, as I did, that these were rough characters and anything could happen, especially on a big-money operation like this.

We puzzled about what to do for a long time. Finally I had an idea. "Why don't I drive my pickup truck to the wharf?" I told Chris Paley. "I'll arrive before the boat docks, and Rod'll take one look, bawl me out, and send me home to get the car. There's no way he's going to let me take the crew to the airport in the pickup."

Chris agreed, and that's exactly what happened. When I arrived at the dock, Rod was already there, pacing around, tense as usual, the hawk face looking everywhere, even at the warehouse. Now he took one look at the truck and said, "Go home and get your car, dummy. I told you to get the car, not the truck."

I said I was sorry and acted sheepish. Rod wasn't mad. As far as he was concerned I just wasn't too bright, and it was easy for me to make such a mistake. I drove off. But instead of going home, I sneaked up on the small side wharf at the harbour where boats take on fuel.

Chris was nowhere around, though he was supposed to guard me throughout the takedown. But I didn't care. After the nineteen months of working alone I felt secure enough, knowing that Elaine and the kids were safe. Besides, I knew that there were dozens and dozens of Mounties hidden in the area — and I wasn't going to miss seeing the action for anything.

•   •   •

As the boat slid into the harbour, Rod prowled around on the dock. On the *Lady Sharell* Scotty Germaine appeared at the bow and threw a line to him. Rod caught it and tied it loosely to the wharf. Ed, the skipper, was still manoeuvring her while Scotty started tossing some kitbags onto the wharf. Then Ed cut the diesel engine.

That was the signal.

Two deafening explosions shattered the morning calm. Every living thing – even the gulls – seemed to freeze as the RCMP tactical team charged, yelling, out of the warehouse right onto the wharf and thundered aboard the *Lady Sharell*. At the same time a Coast Guard cutter that had been quietly lurking in the harbour made a turn around the *Sharell*, cutting off her exit route. In seconds about sixty RCMP officers, who'd been sitting out of sight in cars, buses, and even trucks, filled the wharf and the surrounding area.

The explosions came from artillery simulation bombs, and they were part of the tactical team's well-rehearsed attack routine. The object was to surprise, and it certainly worked. I couldn't quite see the expression on Rod's face as the tac team rushed in because I was just a little too far away to make out his features as he was grabbed and handcuffed. But I'm sure he was in a state of shock. I'm also sure that Rod, Ed and the crew didn't know what hit them, it all happened so quickly. Within seconds they were taken away in cars to the cells in Yarmouth.

But I didn't hang around. I went home, made coffee, and called Elaine on the phone at the Halifax Airport Hotel.

It was six o'clock and they were all still asleep, so it took Elaine a while to pick up the receiver.

"It's all over, babe. I'll be there soon," I told her. I could hear the sigh of relief at the other end.

I sat in my chair with my cup of coffee for about twenty minutes, just staring out over the ocean. I found it hard to believe that it was all over. All of a sudden a man burst into the house, yelling at me: "What the . . . ? We've been looking everywhere for you!"

It was Phil. He was red-faced and out of breath.

"Man, sit down and have a coffee," I said, and we grinned at each other.

"You gave us quite a scare. We've been looking for you everywhere," Phil said, catching his breath as he sat.

"Everything is okay. Don't worry," I said.

CHAPTER ELEVEN

Action at Sea

PHIL BUNDLED ME OFF IN A CAR AND TOOK ME BACK TO THE WHARF where the *Lady Sharell* was tied up. The Mounties were standing around grinning as if they'd won the lottery, and I was a pretty popular guy right then. After the backslaps and handshakes I got taken on a grand tour. Phil took me aboard and showed me the hashish in her hold, which was being unloaded to the dock by a group of Mounties. Ed and the crew had put a blue tarpaulin over the pile of bales so they wouldn't get wet from the ice that was on top. The bales themselves were not too impressive, about two feet by eighteen inches, covered with burlap and loosely tied around with rope, but there were a lot of them. And since each one weighed about sixty pounds, I knew that I was looking at a lot of money.

The Mounties were very pleasant as they showed me around. But I think they were going out of their way to be nice because of a conversation we'd had a few days before the *Lady Sharell* sailed. On Ottawa's instructions – and they made that clear – they took me aside and said: "Look, we have to tell you this: If there's one bale missing, we're holding you responsible."

I was pretty angry. The geniuses at the top still couldn't get it through their heads that I wasn't in this for the money and wasn't part of the drug mob. Did they really think that I'd have done all this for a bale of hashish? After all, from the outset Rod's gang had promised me big money – "We're talking millions," they'd said. Now this stupidity.

Anyway, all the RCMP people on the scene were very friendly as we stood there watching. The whole harbour was still roped-off, holding back crowds of startled Lockeport folks who must have thought a world war had started when the bombs blasted them awake. The Mounties were trying to figure out how to move the piles of dope. Against my advice, they'd brought only one truck, and when they tried to borrow another one from a local man, he wasn't happy about that, and he told them he needed it. "I was really scared that the gang would think I was in the undercover operation with you," he told me later.

While the Mounties were trying to round up another truck, their exhibit man – the guy who catalogues all the evidence for presentation in court – was weighing the *Lady Sharell*'s cargo. With help from the tac team – fit-looking men in dark camouflage fatigues who formed a bucket brigade to toss the bales up on the deck, then from the deck to the dock – Corporal Bryan London carefully weighed each pile of hashish. There were 453 in all, each weighing between fifty and sixty pounds. The total was 26,722 pounds, or 13.361 tons. Its estimated street value was $238 million. It was without

question the largest such seizure in Canada at that time, in
fact the largest drug bust in North America.

.   .   .

No sooner was the crew of the *Lady Sharell* led away than
another drama began way out on the high seas. The Canadian
Forces destroyer *Iroquois*, which had been staying discreetly
out of sight, started to move in on the *Ernestina*. By 10 A.M.
the weather had turned foggy, and visibility was less than one
hundred yards when the *Iroquois'* skipper, Commander Brian
R. Brown, hailed the freighter via the marine radio frequency.

"This is the Canadian warship *Iroquois*. I am one mile off
your starboard beam. You are requested to identify your vessel and stop . . . for the purpose of boarding for inspection."

There was no way that the *Ernestina* could have seen the
warship in the fog. Perhaps for a moment she thought of
running for it. But perhaps her skipper was confident that an
empty hold ("Hashish – what hashish?") would establish her
innocence. She responded almost immediately: "Name ship
Ernestina. Echo, Romeo, November, Echo, Sierra, Tango, In-
dia, November, Alpha. Over."

Brown repeated: "This is the Canadian warship *Iroquois*.
Roger. Over. You are requested to stop your vessel in its
present position for the purpose of boarding and inspection.
Over."

"Okay, one minute," the *Ernestina* shot back. Were they
thinking of running?

Brown, now growing slightly impatient, demanded a straight
answer: "This is the Canadian warship *Iroquois*. What is your
decision with respect to stopping your vessel in the present
position? Over."

"Yes, I stop now. But standby, standby now. Stop after five
minutes," came the *Ernestina*'s response.

"Roger, I will continue to close your position slowly to
attempt to establish visual contact," Brown responded.

The *Iroquois* had received orders to arrest the freighter

only minutes before. The warship had an RCMP task force on board, and neither they nor the navy people really knew how a boarding party would be received by the smugglers. To encourage them to show good manners, thirteen of the crew's best riflemen were assembled into a cover party – a back-up assault team – and positioned on the destroyer's uppermost deck just as the *Iroquois* came within sight of the freighter. The men were told not to point their FNC1 rifles at the *Ernestina*. Just the same, the giant warship breaking out of the fog with her main armaments pointed at the freighter must have been a pretty scary sight for the *Ernestina*'s crew.

Brown used the radio again to say he'd stop his warship off the *Ernestina*'s port beam to put a boarding party in the water, and also asked for the freighter's heading.

All of a sudden a new voice came from the *Ernestina*: "Hello, *Iroquois*. This is the *Ernestina*. I've just been woken up. Can I be of assistance?"

The voice added that the freighter's course was 090 degrees and offered assistance to the boarding party.

After more conversation, a Jacob's ladder appeared down the *Ernestina*'s port side, and the *Iroquois* lowered the first of two inflatable Zodiacs, with four RCMP officers and two navy men aboard. All of them were wearing floater jackets, some with the letters RCMP stencilled on them, and they carried their service .38 Smith and Wesson revolvers in their pockets or their belts. Each of them also carried a specially issued twelve-gauge shotgun, in case things got a little boisterous.

There was a sea on, and even crossing the short fifty-yard gap between the ships, the inflatables were tossed around. But so were the two big ships, especially the *Ernestina*. With her engines shut off, she was at the mercy of the sea, and her crew, ordered by the warship's commander to stay on deck and in sight, had to lean against the superstructure to stay upright.

Commanding the boarding party was Staff Sergeant Lawrence Warren, a twenty-three-year RCMP veteran. He was in the lead Zodiac and first man aboard the *Ernestina*. Before he jumped to climb up the heavy Jacob's ladder, he left his shotgun in the Zodiac. Tucked into his belt, inside his floater jacket and coveralls, he had his service .38. When he vaulted onto the *Ernestina*'s deck he noted that all seven members of the freighter's crew were obediently lined up in the open deck area near the centre of the ship, where they could be seen from the destroyer.

Pulling out his badge, Warren said: "I am Staff Sergeant Warren of the Royal Canadian Mounted Police drug section in Halifax."

Just as formally he went on to tell the crew that they and their ship were under arrest under the provisions of the Narcotics Control Act as well as the Customs Act. They were charged with conspiracy to import narcotics into Canada and with the actual importation of narcotics into Canada, "specifically into Lockeport, Nova Scotia."

After he read them the standard police warning that anything they may say may be used as evidence against them, the only response – and I guess it was a bit of an anti-climax – came from Harry Sunila, who said: "These people don't speak English."

"Are you the captain, sir?" Warren asked him.

"No, this is the captain," he said, pointing at Malik Solayman. Asked the same question, Solayman nodded his head. (Later in court he'd claim that he didn't speak good enough English to understand what Warren was asking him.)

Warren's exchange with the crew took several minutes. As more Mounties poured on board, the crew were handcuffed and taken to the captain's quarters. Each man was identified by matching him up with passports and other documents found on board, and all of the crew were strip-searched.

Sunila did all the translating for Karim and was very polite, making sure to call the policemen "Sir."

Meanwhile, the three Mounties who had followed Warren up the Jacob's ladder – Sergeant Eric Caulder and Constables Ron Robinson and John Fritz – had fanned out to check the ship for additional people or evidence. Robinson and Caulder gave the ship a preliminary going over while Fritz drew his revolver before bursting into the bridge area – only to find it empty.

The Mounties found a navigational aid with co-ordinates marked on it that corresponded almost exactly to the position, five miles off the eastern tip of Sable Island where the *Lady Sharell* had picked up her contraband cargo. They also found a black shoulder bag, which contained some of Captain Sunila's identification papers. As it was being taken to Halifax, another Mountie searched it again and found, carefully folded in a side pocket, fifteen one-thousand-dollar bills in Canadian currency. When the Mounties checked the serial numbers, sure enough they matched up with the bills Rod had given me for Ed to hand over to the mother ship's captain.

Some navy men now boarded the *Ernestina* for what turned out to be a very uncomfortable trip back to Halifax. It took four days, in rough sea, and several of the RCMP people were so affected that they "fed the gulls." There were now thirty-one people aboard, including the original crew, and only seven bunks, so nobody got much sleep. To make matters worse, the navy people had trouble starting the engines and operating the gyro and automatic pilot. Several times they called on Malik Solayman to help, and he did.

After a rough passage, the *Ernestina* was brought to the Canadian Forces Base at Shearwater, where the Mounties again searched her from stem to stern but failed to turn up anything more. They can't have done a great job, because as she was being winterized, a workman found a .38 calibre pistol in a toolbox. It was the one that Karim carried in his belt. Solayman identified it in court, and he went on to guess that the missing Russian machine gun that was so handy for keeping discipline must have been thrown overboard when the *Ernestina* was first hailed by the *Iroquois*.

•   •   •

While I was looking over the *Lady Sharell*'s cargo, her crew, along with Ed — not to forget my friend Tony, who had been grabbed at the stash site when the Mounties charged in from the nearby woods — were being driven to Yarmouth to be charged. Rod, of course, was already a known quantity, thanks to the earlier efforts of Miami DEA agent Billy Yout, who had tracked him for months in order to find out his real name, Rory O'Dare. Tony sullenly gave the last name Busco, which was also phoney, and the DEA soon identified him as Anthony Lautieri, also of Miami.

But in the days immediately following the arrests, the captain of the *Lady Sharell* fascinated them the most. He had complete papers in the name of Ed Knight. Although he had been under surveillance by the Mounties and the DEA ever since he appeared in Nova Scotia at the beginning of March, they'd had no luck in finding out who he really was.

Billy Yout hadn't been able to stay away from the finale of the drama. In Yarmouth he watched the RCMP question the arrested men, but stayed in the background, hoping they'd be caught off-guard. But as Ed calmly stuck to his story that he was Ed Knight, Yout moved in.

"The I.D. that he had just didn't click with me," Yout recalled. "And the Mounties agreed. It was just too neat. I wasn't satisfied with the story.

"We had snatches of information, and I did some checking with our offices, and we came up with a name — Cassidy. We didn't have a picture, but we knew that the case, which in volved hash smuggling in the Carolinas, ended with a father and son being arrested. I decided to try it out on him.

"We had him sitting there, claiming he was Ed Knight. Even though we had fingerprints, by the time we got them back from the United States, he would have been out on bail. So I talked to him. I advised him of his rights even though we were in Canada. It was my intention to bring him back to the United States to stand trial.

"He and the others were all upset about that. When they saw the DEA badge, they knew this wasn't just a local RCMP unit that had just happened to trip over them. I purposely didn't talk to them for a long time to see if we could trip them up. Then I went in there and showed him my badge and credentials, and you could actually see the nervousness on his face."

Yout decided to use an old trick to make Ed believe that the game was up. "I went in with a picture, and it was a picture of just anyone, a picture I'd just picked up in the office. And I said to him: 'What if I was to tell you that I know that you and your son were arrested in the Carolinas and that I've got a picture of you and your son right here? What are you going to say to that?' "

"My name is Ed Knight," he shot back.

"Apparently the son in the Carolinas case was in jail await-ing sentencing, so I said: 'What if I were to tell you that the sentencing of your son is going to be delayed until we I.D. you?' "

There was no reply.

' "OK,' I said, 'I'll leave the picture here, and when you pick that picture up and you see yourself, you'll know that we know who you are. You're going to have to admit to yourself who you are.'

"As I was going out the door – before he lifted the picture up – he said, 'My name is Cassidy.'

"He 'fessed up. Then he picked up the picture, and you should have seen his face!

"Sometimes you have to try things like that," Billy, the good old boy from Florida, laughed, shaking his head.

After that experience, Cassidy promised to co-operate with the DEA. But I guess you won't be surprised to learn that he never came through.

Besides being in jail facing long sentences, Rod and Tony were having problems of their own. Yarmouth jail isn't noted for its vegetarian food, and I heard that they had demanded it and went on a hunger strike when none was provided. I knew that they took the vegetarian stuff very seriously, but the authorities didn't know that and ignored their request.

I'm told that they ended up fasting for days before the warden gave in and provided them with special food.

•   •   •

I wasn't around to see all of Ed's, Rod's, and Tony's problems at first hand. As soon as I finished looking at the *Lady Sharell*'s cargo and received the last handshake from the delighted Mounties, Brent Crowhurst took me through the lines of gaping onlookers and drove me away from Lockeport and on to Halifax to join my family at the Airport Hotel.

On our way we just happened to drive behind a van full of kids from our church going to a convention in New Brunswick. The driver was my brother-in-law Doug, and with him was Elaine's sister Gayla. They already knew about the drug bust and our role in it. We waved excitedly to one another, but Brent didn't stop because I wanted to get to Halifax as fast as possible.

Elaine had called them and her other sister, Betty; I had grabbed a moment to call Jim Dooks. They were all stunned at the thought that I'd been spying on the drug mob for the Mounties for nineteen months, and they'd never seen hide nor hair of the mob or the Mounties. Betty, who depended on Elaine, was very upset and started crying so hard her husband had to calm her down. News travels fast in a small town, and by the time Sharon called her best friend, Patricia, she, too, had heard that something was happening at the Government Wharf and that "Leonard Mitchell's boat was involved."

Brent and I arrived at the Airport Hotel around noon. Sharon, Jewell, and Elaine were out on the lawn waiting for us. Sharon commented at how relieved I looked, and she remembers now that I looked "so different." There were lots of hugs and kisses all around, and I told them all the details, and how Chris and I had our pictures taken together after the bust.

We had a joyous supper at the hotel. It was pretty noisy that night, but we all had a good night's sleep — the first in months for me. In the morning we went to the front desk and picked up all the newspapers. Sure enough, the arrests made headlines in the Halifax papers, and there were a couple of pictures of the bales of hashish being taken off the *Lady Sharell*.

Our euphoria lasted several days. I was proud of the job I had done and gave the RCMP permission to mention how I'd helped – indeed I insisted that they release the details of my role. I knew the mob would know right away, so I thought I might as well get the credit as well as face the danger. Sharon, Jewell, and Elaine were proud of me, too. And I started to look forward to a new adventure under a new name with a bit of ready cash to start some sort of a new business.

CHAPTER TWELVE

Moving into Limbo

IT WAS THE MOUNTIES WHO INSISTED THAT WE COULDN'T GO BACK to Lockeport. I was still a bit shellshocked from the sudden end of my nineteen-month adventure, and I didn't feel like arguing when Brent Crowhurst announced: "We're moving you out. It's too dangerous for you to go back home."

What he said was true. There were 453 bales of hashish in the Mounties' hands to prove that I'd been dealing with big-time crooks, and I didn't need much convincing that whoever backed the gang in Miami wouldn't hesitate to take revenge on me and my family. After all, $238 million was a lot of cash, not even counting the extra bucks spent on the boat refit and other expenses. And I had a hunch that big crime bosses didn't like being outsmarted. They probably liked it even less than ordinary people. The sinister-looking captain of the *Ernestina* and his crew were being held in Halifax, while Rod, Tony, Ed, and the *Lady Sharell*'s deckhands were in custody in Yarmouth, and there were rumours that they might get bail. They all had expensive lawyers, and it looked as if – surprise, surprise – there was an organized effort behind them. I was sure that whoever was backing them wouldn't take too kindly to me and my role in all this.

Sure enough, word came through the underworld grapevine, and the Mounties passed it on to me, that a contract had gone out on my head. Word was passed through Canada's jails that the mob wanted me dead.

That made me glad that I'd received the Mounties' promise that I'd be protected "for a hundred years," if necessary. The other promise was that I'd be "duly compensated." I was relying on them for that, just as I was relying on them to fix up the new identity and the "new life" they'd discussed.

So it was a shock to discover after the takedown that the Mounties didn't have anything arranged for this much-discussed new life. Nothing. Not a thing.

As I looked back on it, I guess I'm partly to blame for not getting it nailed down. I was hoping until the last moment that when it all ended we could simply remain in Lockeport and go on with our lives. I see now that we should have had an exact plan ready, and that Elaine and I should have discussed it thoroughly. But neither of us thought about it very much. I was so obsessed with getting the operation completed that I never considered what would happen afterward. I'd assumed – and this was my big mistake – that the RCMP would work it out for us. Either we'd stay in Lockeport or they'd give us the promised identity change, provide a fair cash settlement, and we'd head off somewhere exciting and do something new. I know now that this was naive of me. Police forces and governments just don't work like that.

We first realized how tough it was going to be to leave Lockeport on the Monday following the arrests. We'd been on a spiritual high during the weekend, ever since I rejoined the family on Saturday at the Airport Hotel. Now we'd come back to Lockeport for the last time to say good-bye to friends and family. You can imagine what it was like going back to our own house with our Mountie bodyguards. The thought that we'd never be able to live in our dream house again and see our family on a daily basis made Elaine and me sad. But the girls were devastated. Sharon remembers crying as if her heart would break as she went into her room: "It was just like a dream. I felt like I was a different person just looking at Sharon's room. It just hit me that we were losing everyone."

The girls had planned to go to the high school after lunch to take their leave of their friends. But there were TV cameras outside the house, and the Mounties for good reasons didn't want the girls' pictures on TV under any circumstances. Brent Crowhurst went outside and spoke to Yvonne Colbert from ATV in Halifax and told her I had done a great job and that he had no other comment. The TV crew left and went over to the girls' high school, where they asked some of the students what they thought of the drug bust. The crew eventually disappeared from sight, but the Mounties remained apprehensive.

It was obvious that the girls couldn't continue with their school year. So Brent went to speak to the principal, who agreed, because they'd both done really well, to give them final marks without requiring them to write exams.

But the parting was very, very hard on them. And the Mounties were so jumpy that the girls might make a slip that they really didn't help. Two of Sharon's friends came over to say good-bye, and Brian, the Mountie who'd been guarding them at the Oak Island Inn, took her aside and said, "Make sure you don't tell them where we're going." Sharon got mad at that. Then she had to forcefully close a door on one of the women Mounties to get some privacy to say farewell to her best friend, Patricia.

Can you imagine saying good-bye to friends and family and not being able to tell them where you were going? That's what Elaine and I had to do, and it was terrible. Elaine's sister

Betty and her daughter Brandys were there at our house along with Jim Dooks and Elaine's other brother, Wayne, who is a minister in Shelburne. Jim was proud of me, but I could see in his eyes that he didn't like the idea of running our business without me. I thought that he could manage, especially if I could help him get going with my promised settlement from the RCMP. That would make all the difference.

But our most moving farewell was yet to come. Elaine's sister Betty assembled our entire family at her house in Shelburne for an early potluck supper. Her house isn't big, and people had to wait on the patio for their turn to come inside, while the Mounties guarded the outside. Brandys, Elaine's little niece, cried until she was hysterical. The scene stuck with us for a long time.

•   •   •

After our farewells our bodyguards took us on a sort of six-week tour around the Maritimes. Our first stop was the Old Orchard Inn, a beautiful resort in Kentville in the Annapolis Valley. The valley is apple-growing country, and it was blossom time, and the air was sweet. I guess I was still in a bit of a daze, but I really managed to relax, and so did Elaine. I found it hard, though. Once, while we were moving around from hotel to hotel with our escort, I just got into the car at Bridgewater late at night and drove to Lockeport to go slowly past our house. Jim Dooks, whom the Mounties had allowed to come up for the day, was along with me. I just wanted to visit the place and smell the sea air. I guess I missed home from the day I left – and I still do.

But we now began to have serious discussions with Brent Crowhurst about our future. It dawned on me for the first time that the Mounties had made no plans for us. Elaine and I were under pressure to come up with a place where we wanted to settle permanently. Brent Crowhurst, Chris Paley, and other Mounties met with us every few days to try to find a place that suited them and us. Lethbridge was mentioned and then Calgary. The appeal of Calgary was that Elaine's brother John was a policeman on the Calgary force, and we'd all been out there to visit, and Sharon had once spent an entire month there with John and his family. Since we couldn't wander indefinitely around the Maritimes, we finally settled on Calgary.

Near the end of my nineteen months of undercover work the Mounties in Yarmouth had worked out a financial settlement for me that seemed fair. I assumed that it was working its way through the bureaucracy and that the money and our change in identity would follow soon. I would still miss Lockeport and the ocean, but at least I could get a new business of some sort started in Calgary. But some odd things were happening. At one point the Mounties insisted that once in Calgary we were to have contact only with Elaine's brother, and not with his family. This was crazy, and Elaine became upset. The Mounties finally agreed that, okay, the family could become part of our lives in Calgary, and we began to feel a lot better about the whole idea.

But we still had to work out a cover story about who we were for the benefit of new people we would meet. We had to have a past. Our real one wouldn't do, because anyone gunning for us could easily find us. Eventually, of course, we'd get a legal change of name and identity, but that would take time, and we had to be able to cope in Calgary as soon as we arrived. In the end Brent Crowhurst and Phil Pitts met with us and announced that when we moved out west, we were to pretend that we were from Prince Edward Island.

If you've never tried to assume another identity you can't imagine how hard it can be, and what kind of difficulties you can get into. Anyone who has read John le Carré's spy novels knows that spies entering foreign countries spend months or even years learning what they call their legends. Of course, we weren't going on a spying mission and wouldn't have to face the tough questioning of counterspies. But a new, fake identity can make a lot of trouble, especially for a family.

From the start Elaine and I weren't happy with the choice of P.E.I. It's nothing against the island, which is a fine place.

But the two of us had been to P.E.I. only briefly, and the children not at all. So the Mounties tried to solve that by giving us a week-long tour of P.E.I. We were accompanied by the two RCMP women constables, Nicole and Karen, while a local RCMP man drove us around and pointed out the sites we'd need to be familiar with in order to pretend to be from there.

He'd say, "Here's the curling rink that you ought to know, and this is the main street," and so on. The girls picked up some travel brochures when we got off the ferry, and we tried to memorize all the place names. The Mounties even took the girls to the schools they were supposed to have attended, and in the junior high school, where Jewell was supposed to have gone, they met the principal.

"If you move here, we'd love to have you," he told Jewell. The Mounties must have told him we were thinking of moving there. Sharon had a walk through the senior high school but talked to no one.

There was one good thing that happened on the trip. On the way to P.E.I. we met Chris Paley – Papa Smurf – who was on holidays with his family in New Glasgow, and for the first time we saw him completely relaxed. We all went out to dinner, Elaine and I and Chris and his wife, while the girls stayed in and ordered pizza and watched movies on TV. We enjoyed Chris, and it was a pleasure to see him again and to remember the things we'd shared.

Our journey took us to New Brunswick, where the girls discovered that the travelling Bill Lynch Fair, which they'd visited often in Nova Scotia, had caught up with us. Brian was once again roped into taking them. The poor man must have been getting tired of it all, because Sharon reported that he became queasy on some of the rides. The girls also got a reminder of reality when his jacket kept riding up over the handgun in his belt. "I've got to get a new jacket," he told them. They should have been scared, but they found it all very glamorous.

I could see now that the Mounties were making a deliberate

effort to keep us out of Nova Scotia because the *Lady Sharell's* crew was now in court in Yarmouth. The papers were giving the case full coverage, and the Mounties felt it just wasn't safe for us to be back in our home province. By this time, unlike the girls, I was getting good and tired of hotel life, and settling in Calgary began to look attractive. In the end we left for Calgary on June 21 – exactly six weeks after we had been forced to leave Lockeport for a new life on the run. Brent Crowhurst was tagged to fly with us, and the girls got to choose one of the four bodyguards to go with us as well. Naturally, they chose Brian.

.   .   .

Our life in Calgary started out all right. We arrived in June and after a short spell at the Delta Bow Valley Inn we settled in a nice one-storey house in a residential neighbourhood. The house was in a cul-de-sac, and the neighbours were friendly – and nosey, and this was to cause us some problems. For a few weeks things were just great. I got my mind and body in shape and the rest did me good. I hadn't felt better in a long, long time. We missed our home, but we also enjoyed our first weeks in Calgary. It's a vibrant new city fuelled by the huge oil boom of the 1970s, and I'll tell you, it was quite a contrast to Lockeport, both in size and spirit. We enjoyed setting up house and buying new furniture.

But as the weeks turned into months and the months wore on, I got more and more restless. By Christmas of 1985, I was just itching to get on with my life, and I was driving Elaine and the kids crazy.

The problem was that I couldn't work. We were using a new name, of course, but our identity hadn't been legally changed. Although the Mounties did help me get a new driver's licence in P.E.I., I couldn't use my credit cards, my social insurance number – anything – and, of course, I couldn't refer to my past business record. So there was no way I could start a new enterprise. To use any of the old documents would have left a trail that the mob could pick up, and I was very mindful of that contract out on my life and didn't feel like taking chances.

So I was stuck at home, sentenced to do nothing. That may sound pretty good, but just try it some time. I was living in limbo on money doled out by the RCMP and not allowed to do anything. I'm hyperactive and just not used to doing nothing, and this was like punishment for me. For months I'd get up and search for something to do. At first I used to work out doing exercises for up to four hours a day in our rec room, using some gym equipment I'd bought, until I was as fit as a fiddle. Then I'd get into the car and drive aimlessly around the city and its outskirts, just looking at the prairie, or the foothills and the Rockies to the west. At least the driver's licence made me mobile.

We joined a church in Calgary and met some nice people there. But we always had to be careful not to talk about the past, and, as you'd imagine, this made social life difficult. I did make some business contacts and became friends with a man named Ernie, who bought and sold used trucks and other vehicles. We used to go together to car auctions, and I would advise him on what to buy. I made no money from it, but it did give me something to do.

Even so, I still spent a lot of time at home, which was soon noticed in the cul-de-sac where we lived. The rest of the men on the street went off to their jobs, and only the women stayed home. Elaine and I told the neighbours that I was in sales, and worked irregular hours. But when they'd drop around for coffee and chat with Elaine, I'd be there, and they'd want to know our whole life history. All of this was tough on us because we were, in effect, living a lie – and one that might not stand up under close scrutiny.

The RCMP paid our mortgage on the house in Lockeport, and we received an allowance in Calgary, which was just barely adequate. It certainly wasn't anywhere near what I used to earn back home, and it was way below what I'd have made in Calgary if I'd been able to operate normally. The promised settlement hadn't materialized by New Year's 1986.

And as the months dragged on, it became harder and harder to explain our existence to people. The neighbours were asking a lot of questions, and on a little blind street like that we couldn't snub them for being curious. Our story about my job in sales must have seemed pretty thin, since I was at home so much. Yet we obviously managed to pay the rent and had a recent-model leased Chevy. This sure set people wondering. What made matters worse was that our Mountie contacts, Earl and Don, brought our allowance once a week. They usually drove a flashy Chrysler New Yorker, and sometimes they'd come in separate cars so there'd be two big fancy cars parked in front of our house. They always wore suits and dark glasses to come in and spend some time with us. They were very nice people, but we didn't have the close relationship with them that we had with Chris Paley and Brent Crowhurst back in Nova Scotia.

There were even more raised eyebrows on the street when our leased Chevy gave us trouble and the RCMP provided us with a New Yorker rent-a-car. For a while we had a different rented car just about every week, usually a flashy one. Our neighbours could see that we didn't have any money to throw around, and they took notice of the cars. One of them asked Sharon, "Why does your father drive a rented car?" Another time, when the two Mounties arrived, the woman for whom Sharon was babysitting said "My, your mother's got a lot of company today" and waited for Sharon to tell her who the men were. These were silly incidents, but they were making it very difficult for us to cope.

Our cover story of being from Prince Edward Island was also causing us difficulty. The RCMP forgot that the boom in Alberta had attracted many people from Eastern Canada, and Elaine and I would constantly run into people from P.E.I.

"What part of the island are you from?" they'd ask excitedly, and they'd start mentioning names of streets and names of people and say that their son still lived there and that their mother-in-law just came in yesterday for a visit. We had to field these questions as well as we could. People would also phone Elaine and say, "Hey, my kid's doing a project on Prince Edward Island. Maybe you can tell us something." And Elaine would fudge it as best she could, putting them off or saying, "We've got something here somewhere. Let me look." Then she'd pretend that the stuff got lost in the move or in the packing.

Sharon had the hardest time with the P.E.I. story. Once she was asked in school who the premier of P.E.I. was, and she was terrified when she didn't know. That and problems in understanding the computerized report card she'd got from a large high school in Charlottetown left her fretting: "I thought they would catch me by any mistake I made."

I don't know why the Mounties gave us such a complicated background story. They should have picked something that was more familiar to us, someplace we had lived. In fact, thinking about it, we could have even kept our own name and just changed the story slightly. Mitchell is a common enough name – in Calgary the most famous is W.O. Mitchell, the novelist – and the drug bust didn't get much coverage out west.

The worst thing about the Calgary experience was the feeling of isolation. The whole family felt it. Sure, we had Elaine's brother John nearby, and he and his family couldn't have been nicer. But Elaine missed her sisters and her nieces, especially Brandys, and they couldn't even call us. "It was hard. Really hard. I was very lonely for the rest of my family and was feeling more and more cut off," she recalled later.

It was also hard for us not to see Chris Paley, Phil Pitts, and Brent Crowhurst. They'd become very important people in our lives, Chris and Phil during my many months of undercover work and Brent during the six weeks following the arrests. We had come to depend on them a great deal, and now, all of a sudden, we weren't even allowed to talk to them. I suppose that was standard procedure with the Mounties, but I didn't like it. To be fair, the Mounties didn't abandon us completely. There were Don and Earl, who not only delivered our allowance but were supposed to help us in case of difficulty. And the Calgary officers were also extremely busy – one was on the RCMP homicide squad and the other dealt with tax evasion cases – so we knew we were just something extra added to their caseload. It would have been good if we could have discussed with them how to deal with the various problems we faced in our everyday life and found out what the future held for us.

As time went on, we felt ourselves at the mercy of the RCMP establishment. We just couldn't understand why we couldn't have contact with Brent and Chris, and we began to suspect that the Mountie establishment had something up its sleeve. We did call Chris and Brent from time to time, but the local contacts in Calgary made it clear that they didn't like it, and this made us even more suspicious. "What are they up to?" Elaine and I wondered.

·   ·   ·

What they were up to was not paying me the settlement I thought we'd agreed on months ago. Before we left Nova Scotia, the Yarmouth detachment had my business evaluated and proposed a financial settlement to compensate me for the loss of the scrapyard and the other businesses which I'd built up over the years, as well as for the need to change our identity, and the loss of my ability to make a living. It was a good sum of money, but I thought the money was fair. I can't disclose the actual figure, but I wasn't embarrassed by the size of it. As the months dragged on while I was not able to work – our legal change of name hadn't come through either – I felt the amount that had been set was barely fair.

But funny things began to happen. The Yarmouth RCMP detachment, the guys who'd worked with me and knew what I'd done, recommended the payment of the agreed-upon sum, but the top command in Halifax had changed, and the new people there cut the amount to less than half.

I couldn't believe it. It seemed that they treated murderers better than honest citizens – the RCMP had paid Clifford Olson a hundred thousand dollars to show them where he'd buried the bodies of his victims – and I was hurt and disappointed. We were now locked in a nasty money dispute. I wanted what I'd been promised. After all, I lost my business, and by their own description I'd done an excellent job for them. But what got us all down was the fact that as far as our new identity was concerned, we were in limbo.

Despite the arguments and appeals I made both in Calgary and by phoning Brent and Chris back in Nova Scotia, I got nowhere. I knew that the individual Mounties weren't monsters and that our difficulties were caused by a bureaucratic tangle. Sure, we were in a financial dispute of some size, but it seemed to me at that time – and it still does – that if they'd moved faster on our change of identity, I'd have gotten back to work much quicker and my financial loss would have been much less. I was very disappointed that no one at a high level in Ottawa cut through the red tape and ended our problems. I was getting quite frustrated because I felt I'd put out a great deal for this enterprise exposing myself and my family to danger, and now this was the thanks I was getting.

CHAPTER THIRTEEN

The Aftermath

I FULLY EXPECTED TO BE CALLED AS A WITNESS AT THE TRIAL OF the smuggling gang. And while I wasn't looking forward to it, I saw it as part of the job. As it turned out, the evidence in the case was so strong that I was never called. Rod, Ed, Tony, and the three crewmen from Florida all pleaded guilty in provincial court in Yarmouth, after being held in jail for almost exactly a month. The Crown attorneys and the smugglers' lawyers had been busy during the month and managed to make a deal that the six men would plead guilty to one charge each. In return, the Crown agreed to drop additional charges.

I don't know whether the gang expected light sentences in return. If they did, they must have been disappointed. Rod

– or Rory Paul O'Dare – pleaded guilty to conspiring to import narcotics into Canada and was sentenced to nine years in prison. Ed – John Frederick Cassidy – received seven years on the same charge. Tony, whose full name was Anthony Raymond Lautieri, received eight and a half years after pleading guilty to importing narcotics. The three crewmen, Maurice Germaine, David Tuthill, and Robert Barnett, were each sentenced to five years on charges of possessing a narcotic for the purpose of trafficking.

They were whisked off to various jails and penitentiaries, and I never saw any of them again. The only message I got from any of them came from Ed, the one I liked the best out of the whole bunch. He said to a Mountie, who passed it along, "Tell Leonard that I don't understand why he did it."

We had just arrived in Calgary when all this took place, and I heard later that they all took the sentences without showing any emotion, except for Tony, who was very upset and dropped his head on Rod's shoulder in despair.

As for the *Lady Sharell*, she ended up with the shipyard where we had had the first refit done. They had seized her under a mechanic's lien because Rod had held back part of the final payment after we had all the problems.

•   •   •

The case of the *Ernestina*'s crew was more complicated. Initially all seven crewmen were arrested and charged. But only Harry Sunila and Malik Solayman, who claimed he was a law student, faced a Canadian court. The other five, including Abdul Karim, had the proceedings against them stayed and were deported in mid-June, less than a month after the arrests. The thinking on the part of the authorities was that since the crewmen were foreigners, they'd be deported if they were convicted anyway, so there was no point in wasting money on a trial. But Billy Yout, the u.s. Drug Enforcement Agency agent, was startled that the crewmen were let go so quickly, since not having them as prospective witnesses weakened any case he might have had in the United States. "You always keep your witnessess around until the trial goes," Yout said. "Then if you want to deport them, you deport them afterwards." He said neither he nor the DEA were consulted. "I think the decision was made by the RCMP hierarchy." As it turned out, there were no indictments in the United States, since it would have exposed me and my family to great risk. I'd have had to testify in grand jury proceedings and at trials that might have gone on for weeks.

Yout was also annoyed that the RCMP wouldn't allow him to bring in the American television networks to cover the story of the arrests. "First they said 'okay,' and then they changed their minds," he said, which was infuriating because he'd already arranged with NBC and Cable Network News to have crews stand by in Boston, and they were hot to trot. But then the RCMP said no, that was off, and the bust, the largest in North American history at the time, received major coverage only locally in Halifax and in the *Miami Herald*.

In January 1986 I was flown to Halifax for part of the month-long trial of Solayman and Sunila. The RCMP put me in a guarded motel room – not the Holiday Inn this time – in case I was needed as a witness, but I never had to be called. Crown prosecutor James Bissel took the court through the entire voyage of the *Lady Sharell* and its meeting with the *Ernestina* off Sable Island with the help of a parade of witnessess ranging from Paley and Pitts to the skipper of the destroyer *Iroquois* and Captain Ed himself, who managed to avoid giving too many details of the offloading operation. The Crown had tried to establish that Solayman was the captain of the *Ernestina*. The prosecutor argued that Solayman had helped the navy get the ship going when she was boarded by the RCMP and seamen from the *Iroquois* and had shown a great deal of technical knowledge about the ship. But the jury of six men and six women – who deliberated for two days – believed his story, told through interpreters, that he was a law student working at a summer job and that he knew neither the ship's destination nor the nature of the cargo. He was found not guilty. Sunila, who didn't take the witness stand, was found guilty of importing narcotics and possession for the purpose of trafficking and was sentenced to ten years in prison. Mr Justice A.M. MacIntosh noted that the charge of importing carries a maximum sentence of life imprisonment, as does the possession for trafficking charge, which also calls a mandatory seven-year minimum. He handed down the ten-year sentence for the first charge and added another eight years for the second conviction. But "because the two offences are so closely related," MacIntosh made the sentences concurrent.

My name had come up at the trial, and the Crown wanted me around in case I had to take the stand. I was glad to be back in Halifax, smelling the salt air, but as soon as it became clear that I wouldn't be needed as a witness, I flew back to Calgary. We still didn't have our new legal identity, and there was still no sign of the settlement, though the Mounties kept saying it would be coming soon.

●   ●   ●

Another problem was nagging at Elaine and me. Back in Shelburne, Jim Dooks – a hard worker but short on business savvy – was having a rough time running the business. He'd joined Shelburne Scrap and Metal at my urging after leaving the army, had invested his savings and his army pension money in the business, and now it was going under. The company was some fifty thousand dollars in the hole, and the bank had refused to extend any more credit. The overdraft alone stood at thirty thousand.

I was in touch with Jim by phone and fully in the picture and giving as much useful advice as I could, but there was little I could do to salvage the business other than pump some of my RCMP compensation money into it – once I got it. Jim told me that back in June, right after the bust, the RCMP had brought a Halifax scrap dealer named Norman Ross down to evaluate the business. He'd looked around, examined the profit and loss statement, and confirmed that we were making money. "It was a nice little operation," he told the Mounties.

During the summer, Jim had met several times with Sergeant Brent Crowhurst, who kept assuring him that compensation was on the way. On one occasion Brent came to the scrapyard and promised Jim (in the presence of the company's bookkeeper, Jim MacDougall) that Shelburne Scrap and Metal would be compensated for the losses incurred because of me and that the RCMP would continue to look after me.

Jim's conversations with Crowhurst went on all summer and, according to Jim, Brent would keep telling him to hold on. On one occasion he called and said, "Listen, just hold on for one more month, thirty days, and I might have some good news for you." But after thirty days no money was forthcoming, and by the end of September, after a depressing trip to the bank, Jim told Crowhurst that he would go public with the story of how he was left high and dry by the RCMP because of my undercover work. It must have been tough on Brent, and I'm sure he felt badly about how things were turning out. When he asked Jim to wait another fourteen days before going public, Jim promised to hold off until October 15. Jim later told me that on the fifteenth, Crowhurst called him and said, "There's no money. I've done all I could."

Sadly, Jim closed down the business, selling the equipment and the land to pay off the debts. He didn't get enough for it to cover all the debts and still owed several thousand dollars to creditors. When he took a job at a bottle and metal depot, his salary wasn't enough to cover his mortgage, so the Dooks had to sell their house. All this didn't make us feel any better, or any more pleased with the Mounties.

Jim stuck to his threat to go public. He and his wife, Carol, gave a number of interviews about their plight. Someone sent us a videotape of one interview, with Yvonne Colbert of ATV, the CTV affiliate in Halifax. We also learned that Jim had been contacted by the CTV newsmagazine program "W5," which is seen across the country. I didn't really want him to tell the story on national television, and I tried to talk him out of it when we talked on the telephone.

I was afraid his going public might be dangerous for us, and we were upset enough living in our own strange twilight zone in Calgary. But I never told him flatly not to do it. Jim, of course, didn't know where we were living. In order to phone me he'd contact Brent Crowhurst, who would then call me and I would, in turn, return Jim's call. One day in February Jim phoned me using that route and asked whether I'd make a statement to "W5" about the financial dispute. He sounded very nervous. As soon as I put down the receiver, I said to Elaine and the girls, "I think the 'W5' people were there." My hunch was right. When we watched the story a couple of weeks later, I realized that the program had filmed Jim talking to me on the telephone.

Superintendent Rod Stamler, the RCMP's drug enforcement chief, was also interviewed on the program. He took the line that there was no commitment by the RCMP to Jim or his family and a compensation and protection commitment extended only to me. Jim's problem was with me, not with the RCMP, Stamler said.

"We have no obligation to Mr Dooks. We don't have any moral obligation." But he stopped just short of saying that the Mounties had settled with me. The RCMP was continuing to protect me "in the manner which we undertook at the outset . . . and there is no disagreement between Mr Mitchell and the RCMP," he added.

Jim Dooks's story on "W5" did not endanger our security – we'd been worried about that – and I found myself hoping that it might speed up a settlement, now that Jim had focussed public attention on his plight. Seeing the familiar sights in Shelburne on TV also made us homesick, and a few months later I asked the RCMP whether we could go home on a visit, and to my great surprise, they agreed. It was a joyful occasion, and we saw Jim and Carol Dooks and the rest of Elaine's clan, with several undercover Mounties guarding us all the time. The arrangement was that we would stay only a few days, and I felt very vulnerable. Before I left, I got a demonstration of just how much I depended on the Mounties.

I decided to stay on for a couple of days after Elaine and the children returned to Calgary, but the RCMP didn't want me to. They said they'd withdraw security from me if I stayed on and tried to get me to sign a document acknowledging that I would have no security. I refused to sign, but they withdrew security anyway, for one day and one night, plenty of time for me to keep thinking about that contract that was supposed to be out on me. Bitterly, I recalled the Mounties telling me during the operation that I would have security as long as I needed, "even for a hundred years," as one of them had put it. Fortunately nothing happened to me, but it shook me up and it was a clear attempt to show me just how much I needed the Mounties.

.   .   .

Back in Calgary we faced the worst period of our exile. I'd have given almost anything to resume a normal life and be free of the RCMP and the guys in the suits who brought us our weekly subsistence allowance. Our lack of independence was getting to me. Just how we were kept dangling like puppets by the RCMP was really driven home to me when we had to move our household in mid-July 1986, fourteen long months since the arrests. We'd known for months that our twelve-month lease would end in July, and so we found a slightly bigger house a few streets away. The rent was marginally more, and we advised the RCMP about it. So far so good. I ordered the movers, and on the day I'd arranged the truck came and our furniture was loaded. Like movers the world over, the driver expected to be paid cash on the spot. Then our RCMP contact arrived and told us that the higher echelons had not gotten around to approving our move. So the driver, now worried about being paid said, "Let's unload all the stuff and I'll come back another day." I talked him out of it, and the furniture sat on the truck for a couple of hours while my family waited at our new home for it to arrive. Eventually the approval came, but the episode humiliated me. And as you'd expect, it made me determined to get back to work as soon as possible and away from this bureaucratic nonsense.

Each week when the Mounties came by they'd say, "We're

expecting the settlement next week." They repeated the statement week after week, but nothing happened.

"It's too awful to describe those few months when the RCMP kept saying that it would soon be over," Sharon remembers. "It bothered me to such a degree that one day when Mom was very upset I did something I wasn't supposed to do – I called my aunt Betty in Lockeport. I don't know what I thought I was doing because I was crying so hard that I couldn't even talk. I did blurt out, 'Mom can't stand much more of this. Her nerves are really bad.' Aunt Betty said: 'Where are you? I'll be right there.'

"I didn't tell her where we were before I hung up, and she told Mom a few months later that she had become hysterical and her husband had to calm her down."

The girls – but especially Sharon – suffered a great deal during our Calgary stay and found it really difficult to cope with the secrecy about our past life. They were afraid to make close friends because they'd have to lie to them, and they didn't feel comfortable with that. To make matters worse, Sharon had to change high schools for Grade 12, and we enrolled her in the giant William Aberhart High School. I was still in Nova Scotia on that summer visit, and I remember that she called me three or four times one night, crying and pleading with me not to make her go.

"You've got to go to school," I told her, hoping once she went she'd get over the crisis. The next morning she was brave about it and got a ride with the father of a boy down the road. But she broke down as soon as she got there.

"I fell right to pieces in the school. I started crying right in the hallway, and I was taken home," she recalled. She went on to have terrible nightmares involving guns and hostages.

We didn't send Sharon back to the high school. She found the pressure of changing to the large school just too much, and to cope with the pressures of living in limbo we even sought help from a family therapist. But the sessions weren't much use because we could tell the therapist only the basic outlines of our story, and I guess this made it difficult for her to be of much help. Elaine and Sharon went to see one of the pastors at our church, and he suggested that she go to Bible school, which she did. She decided to take her Grade 12 by correspondence, but to this day hasn't written her exams. She's all right now, and I'm sure she'll get around to getting her high school certificate soon.

The high school incident was the only time she blamed me for what was happening to her. "If it wasn't for you, Dad, I wouldn't be in this mess anyway," she blurted out. She was right, of course. It was my undercover agent work that had landed my family in this mess, and I felt rotten.

•   •   •

It was now time to take some drastic action. I decided to contact the media to tell our story, and I also decided to get a really good lawyer to see whether he could help me break the logjam with the RCMP. I liked the story "W5" did with Jim Dooks, so I telephoned researcher Fiona Fallon at the "W5" Toronto office. Fiona had gone to Shelburne to do the initial research on Jim's story, and he had been very impressed with her. She agreed to meet me at the coffee shop of the Westbury Hotel on Toronto's Yonge Street. She turned out to be a detail-minded, enthusiastic woman in her late thirties and listened to the basic outline of our story – from the Montreal fish deal all the way to our present plight. It had never been made public before, and her bosses assigned her to go ahead with it. I didn't reveal what city we were staying in, but agreed to stay in touch with her by telephone.

I also engaged Robert Rueter of the Toronto law firm Stikeman, Elliott to handle my negotiations with the RCMP. A lanky, youngish-looking man with horn-rimmed glasses and a receding hairline, Rueter proved to be a good friend as well as an excellent lawyer, and he took off after a settlement with the RCMP. At first he didn't want me to tell my story on "W5." But after months of getting the old runaround from the RCMP and the Justice Department in Ottawa, he told me that I probably had nothing to lose by going public.

165

In negotiations with Peter Rehak, executive producer of "W5", I agreed that Elaine and I would tell our story through an interview and that we would be disguised. Producer Don McQueen and reporter Dennis McIntosh, who had done the story on Jim Dooks, were naturals for the story, and it was soon agreed that Elaine and I would have our looks altered by stage makeup and that our voices would be disguised.

Even with these precautions, Elaine and I were a bit uneasy. Going on "W5" was a desperate and possibly dangerous move. But we both felt we had to do it, since the Mounties seemed likely to "next week" us to death. "W5" scheduled a weekend early in October for the interview, and we flew to the Harbour Castle Hilton on Toronto's waterfront. For security reasons, "W5" decided to use the show's regular makeup artist. She's a very competent person, but she was completely spooked when she found out that our lives might be in danger if we were recognized, and the interview had to be postponed. But Dennis McIntosh, Don McQueen, and Fiona Fallon used the weekend to grill us about the details of our story. They pieced it together and after interviewing me and Elaine three weeks later I travelled with them while they filmed their report at the scene of my adventure in Shelburne and Lockeport. We also flew to Miami where I was startled by the grandeur of Rod's house. I could now see for myself the fruits of his ill-gotten gains. I also for the first time met Billy Yout. It was a peculiar situation. He had often seen me in Nova Scotia while working on the case with the RCMP but he had always stayed out of sight and I had no idea what he looked like. Now, Fiona Fallon arranged for us to meet and I spent about an hour telling him about our plight. He just kept shaking his head and said he would check out whether I could get compensation from the DEA. He told me it would involve documenting my role since only the Mounties had files on me and I was not keen to have my picture and other details in the DEA files. I was still hoping the RCMP would come through.

The interview with us had to be put off for three weeks because I was scheduled to have the second part of my stomach stapling operation. You'll remember I'd had the first part way back before we even bought the *Lady Sharell*, and the new operation was to complete the process. Believe it or not, the operation caused another problem with the RCMP. As it turned out, the Alberta provincial health plan had stopped paying for this type of operation on October 1, and I was scheduled to go under the knife on October 7. I asked the RCMP to pay the surgeon's fee, arguing that if I'd been back in Nova Scotia, where the health plan covered the operation, it wouldn't have cost me a dime.

The surgeon's fee was $800 and the anaesthetist cost $350, and we simply didn't have that kind of cash. We really had to fight hard before the RCMP agreed to pay for the surgeon, while we had to pick up the fee for the anaesthetist. Even then the decision was made only a day or so before I went under the knife. Like all such dealings with the Mounties, it was a struggle. In Elaine's words: "Everything was like that. You always had to worry to the last minute whether you'd be able to go through with it or not."

The operation was a success. There were none of the complications that followed the first one, and in mid-November we flew back to Toronto to be interviewed by "W5". This time Don McQueen had set up two videotape cameras in the Four Seasons Hotel. For our makeup "W5" had hired experienced theatrical makeup artists, two sisters. For security reasons they were kept in a separate room and were not told what the story was about. They spent a couple of hours on each of us, making us look like completely different people – it was really amazing. Dennis McIntosh took us through the story while our lawyer, Robert Rueter, watched on the sidelines for any legal implications. He also vetted the story before it went to air. When we all watched it together in the "W5" offices, Elaine and I got homesick seeing pictures of our house and the South Shore on the television screen.

McIntosh and McQueen set up the story by using a clip from Prime Minister Mulroney's "war on drugs" speech of a few months earlier. "Drug abuse has become an epidemic which undermines our economic as well as our social fabric," Mulroney said. At the very end, McIntosh reminded everyone that the Mounties had paid the murderer Clifford Olson a hundred thousand dollars and also noted: "The drug seizure on the *Lady Sharell* was the largest hashish haul in North American history. And we can find no record of anyone like Leonard Mitchell staying undercover so long at a risk to him and his family . . . And yet, they cannot reach a settlement with the RCMP . . . While Prime Minister Mulroney is proposing a war on drugs, Leonard Mitchell and his family have fought the war and lost."

·   ·   ·

I suppose it was dumb of me to think that our disguised faces and voices would keep us safely anonymous. Anyone who knew us in Calgary and saw the story on "W5" could probably figure out who we were, or at least start to suspect the truth. I knew I was taking a chance by going public, but we were desperate. Just the same, I wasn't prepared for being recognized. It didn't take long. The story was broadcast on November 23. A day or so afterward I went with Ernie to Calgary City Towing to pick up a truck for an auction, and a fellow who worked there came up to me and handed me a piece of paper with the name Leonard Mitchell written on it. "Do you recognize this fellow?" he asked. That threw a scare into me and we left. Soon afterward I realized that many people in our church had worked out that we were the disguised people in the "W5" story. It was a fairly large congregation – about five hundred people – and that meant that word would go through the city. That shook us up and I called the RCMP. Our contact there said: "We can't tell who knows, or whether word is going to reach the underworld. You better pack a few things and go to the hotel."

We went to the Delta Bow Valley Inn, and Don, one of our regular contacts, met us there. We were about to go to our room when he said, "You better sit down." I knew that something was up. Don went off up to the rooms and returned a short while later, saying, "There's no point in staying. My superiors don't think you're at risk."

He added a little embarrassed: "I'm sorry, but you'd better go home. They don't want you to stay here. They don't think it's a risk." I could see from his face that he wasn't convinced that the line he had given us was true, but there was nothing else we could do except go home. The message was obvious. The RCMP brass were mad because I'd gone on television, and they were going to teach us a lesson. I called Robert Rueter, who was working feverishly to negotiate a settlement. Since we had gone public, things were looking a bit better in that area.

Alarmed at the number of people in Calgary who had apparently recognized us, and hoping that our settlement was near, on December 3 we jammed into a camper I'd purchased through Ernie and took off for Toronto. I called the Mounties a few days after we left Calgary just to check in with them. They advised us not to go to Nova Scotia and I promised that I wouldn't. And that was that. I'd had it with the "next week" guys. As we drove across the wintry prairies, I kept phoning Robert Rueter to see whether the settlement was coming.

It wasn't. But finally — eighteen months after the great Lockeport takedown — we received our new identity papers. That gave a great boost to our spirits, since we were now free to move and could even think of leaving Calgary permanently.

．　　　．　　　．

I didn't find out until later, but while we were travelling our story had reached the House of Commons. The Opposition parties had seen our story on "W5," and Bob Rueter had been actively trying to catch the attention of anyone in politics who would listen. On December 4, a day after we left Calgary, Solicitor General James Kelleher, the minister responsible for the RCMP, appeared before the House of Commons Standing Committee on Justice and the Solicitor General. Svend Robinson, the NDP justice critic, asked Kelleher what action he was prepared to take in our case. He said that the treatment we had received "certainly does raise very serious questions about the application of the Witness Protection Program by the present government."

Kelleher replied that it was government policy not to disclose names of people like myself, but that since I had elected to go on national television, he felt removed from that constraint. "I certainly want to take this opportunity publicly to say that we admire what he did. He did indeed render a very valuable service to Canada, and we certainly commend citizens like him." It was the first high-level public recognition I had received for my undercover role, and it sounded promising.

Kelleher added that an assistant deputy minister of justice was now negotiating with my lawyer and that this had happened even before the "W5" program went on the air. That sounded promising, too. Best of all, Kelleher also added that it was the government's intention "to see that he [Mr Mitchell] receives fair compensation."

A few days later, on December 16, RCMP Commissioner Robert Simmonds appeared before the same committee. This time Robert Kaplan, the Liberal Party critic and a former solicitor general, brought up our case, putting the commissioner on the hot seat.

"First of all," the commissioner said, "I would like to acknowledge that the man was tremendously useful, and he certainly was helpful in a major case. I am disappointed to see disagreement in a sense." But then he got into the official RCMP line, which was that I'd already received a lot of money and there had never been "any direct promises at all" regarding compensation. "Those promises cannot be made at low levels in the organization." He said the RCMP was trying to determine "exactly what the extent of discussion may have been at those levels, though, that could have caused some false impressions."

I was glad I wasn't there to hear him, because I would have been too angry to keep quiet. While I did receive relatively large sums of money over what was now turning into a three-and-a-half-year period – and these were *long* years – most of it covered direct expenses connected with the venture, such as the fishing licence.

Simmonds did grudgingly concede that our identity change "could have been done slightly more expeditiously" than the eighteen months it took. He then explained that it takes a long time, because provincial governments have to be consulted and "we have to file all kinds of certificates."

He did admit, however, that "in this particular case there was considerable delay. Perhaps we could have pushed it a little harder, when you look back at it, and speeded it up a bit." He said most of the delays were not caused by bad faith but by the system. "The system" was a poor excuse for all those months my family and I had spent in limbo in Calgary.

Early in 1987, three years and four months since O'Carroll and Rod and the others had made me an offer I couldn't refuse, we finally settled with the RCMP. Elaine and I got to meet Superintendent Rod Stamler, who turned out to be quite a pleasant fellow in person, and with Robert Rueter's help we arrived at a settlement. It was a relief, but it meant another move. There was no way we could have stayed in Calgary after all the publicity.

I can't tell you where we're living now, for obvious reasons, but we've found peace and happiness at last. Elaine and Sharon and Jewell and I have all been affected by our experience, but I think we're better for it. We met many people who opened their hearts to us when we were in distress, and none of us regret my part in the drug caper.

I feel in my heart it was the right thing to do.

Afterword
By
Peter Rehak

> Direct intercourse with the authorities was not particularly difficult then, for well organized as they might be, all they did was to guard the distant and invisible interests of distant and invisible masters, while K. fought for something vitally near to him.
>
> —Franz Kafka, *The Castle*.

WHEN I FIRST MET LEONARD MITCHELL AT HIS LAWYER'S OFFICE in Toronto, he and his family were at the lowest ebb in their adventure; they were caught in the Kafkaesque situation of having their life controlled by omnipotent authorities which seemed benevolently disposed toward the hero of a major drug bust, but at the same time seemed content to leave him and his family dangling in uncertainty. The Mitchells were in limbo – their change of identity had gotten lost in the bureaucracy, making it impossible for Leonard to work and resume a normal life. At the same time, the Mounties had reneged on their promised financial compensation, leaving Mitchell both hurt and frustrated.

I knew the basic outlines of their story, and the injustice of their situation bothered me. I could not understand why after he had played superspy for the Mounties with much initiative, enthusiasm, and guts, the RCMP and the government could not get their act together, give him a new identity, and settle the financial disagreement. After all, the drug operation had been an undisputed success for the RCMP. Yet no one in the force's senior management, or in the government, seemed to care that the Mitchells' situation bordered on the desperate.

Leonard Mitchell struck me as a proud and determined man, athletic-looking, exuding pent-up energy and down-to-earth honesty. He wanted to tell his story to "W5," hoping that the exposure on national television would push the RCMP and the government into action. As the executive producer of "W5," I wanted the story (you don't often get a chance to get inside North America's major drug bust!), but I was concerned about the effects for the Mitchells of going public. As the book tells, it did briefly make their life difficult, even though they appeared in disguise, but I am convinced that the attention focussed on their plight by "W5" speeded up a settlement.

Since I got to know the Mitchells quite well, working with them on the television program, and then on this book, I can testify that they are unlikely undercover agents. Deeply religious, they are born-again Christians and live by the principles of their faith, which explains their instant and total abhorrence of drugs. Yet Leonard is also a man who can be fiercely competitive in business, loves the intricacies of a deal, and drives himself hard to complete whatever he sets out to do. That is why it mattered to him so much to see the drug caper through to the end.

Leonard is a proud man, proud of what he did as an honest citizen helping the police. He wanted to tell his story in a book because he never got a chance to do so in court; the evidence he gathered was so strong that he didn't have to testify.

I spent considerable time interviewing Leonard and Elaine and their daughters, Sharon and Jewell. With Leonard I toured some of the sites of his adventure, and since he obviously could not witness every single aspect of the operation, I've also drawn on other sources. For example, the transcripts of the month-long trial of the captain and crewman of the *Ernestina* provided graphic details of the action at sea; Billy Yout, the colourful U.S. Drug Enforcement Administration agent, was generous with his time and with useful background information; and the background on the drug trade in Lebanon was provided by Chris Wenner, a daring British television journalist, who filmed the drug clans in the Bekaa Valley. I decided to change the names of the two men who came to Mitchell for the original fish deal and of the organized crime figure in Montreal to avoid needless legal complications. All of the other names and events are real.

The RCMP officers with whom Mitchell worked declined to be interviewed.

I'd like to thank my colleagues who did the story for "W5" and gave me a solid base for my own research – Fiona Fallon, Don McQueen, and Dennis McIntosh. Thanks are also due to my agent, Beverley Slopen, who from the start never wavered in her enthusiasm for the project, and to Doug Gibson, my editor and publisher, who ably steered me through my first venture into hard covers.

PETER REHAK
Toronto, June, 1988